Margaret Whitman Blair

The Roaring 20

The First Cross-Country Air Race for Women

MARGARET WHITMAN BLAIR

NATIONAL GEOGRAPHIC

WASHINGTON, D.C.

· · · DEDICATION · · ·

Dedicated to my teenaged girlfriends: Rori Cremer; Orawan Gardner; Alex and Nina Paraloglou; Rachel and Elana Levine; Chanel, Chantelle, and Charelle Prince. You are the next generation of women and I have high hopes for you. Louise Thaden, in a note she wrote to her friend Mary Berry Preston back in 1929, expressed exactly what I would like to say to all of you:

"Hope you fly higher—longer—and faster than my small efforts. Wishing you every success," and happiness too.

· · · ACKNOWLEDGMENTS · · ·

Special thanks to the following: Lester Reingold, a friend from my WIW days with expertise in aviation as well as a gifted writer, who looked over this manuscript; Tom Mann, another WIW friend who helped me with my research at the Library of Congress, with his usual dedication and sense of fun; Pat Thaden Webb, the next generation of Thaden pilots, whose loving enthusiasm about her mother was contagious; Gene Nora Jessen, who knows so much about the Powder Puff Derby that she wrote a book about it that was as helpful to me as she was; the late Fay Gillis Wells, pioneer pilot, an amazing, gutsy, and lovely lady I was privileged to know and an inspiration for this book; Dennis Wrynn, who first told me about Fay and how to contact her; Doris Rich, another amazing, gutsy woman whose knowledge of early pilots and races was a boon; Melissa Herman, my public relations-minded flyer friend who never let me give up on this project; my editor, Jennifer Emmett, who championed this book through its long and arduous journey; and of course thanks to my better half, Bob Blair, who helps give me courage and steadfastness of purpose through all the ups and downs of this writer's life.
Thanks to all of you.

Book Design by David M. Seager.
The body text is set in Bodoni. The display text is Cocktail Shaker.
Printed in Belgium

Library of Congress Cataloging-in-Publication Data
Blair, Margaret Whitman.
The Roaring Twenty : the first cross-country air race for women / by Margaret Whitman Blair.
p. cm.
Includes bibliographical references and index.
1. Powder Puff Derby—History—Juvenile literature. 2. Women air pilots—United States—History—Juvenile literature.. I. Title.
GV759.2.P74B53 2006
797.5'2'0820973—dc22
2005005472
Trade ISBN: 0-7922-5389-2
Library Binding ISBN: 0-7922-

TITLE PAGE: August 18, 1929, Clover Airfield, Santa Monica, California: The women racers line up their planes for the start of the race. In the foreground (number 100) is Bobbi Trout's Golden Eagle Chief.

· · · CONTENTS · · ·

Foreword

The women you're going to meet in this book had little in common in their backgrounds. What they did have in common was the incredible desire and determination to earn their right to take part in the development of aviation. They didn't take "no" for an answer.

In 1929, women pilots were battling to be accepted in the field of aviation. This first major cross-country race for women was the golden opportunity to prove that women were as competent to fly as men, and to prove to a nervous public that airplanes and long-distance flying were going to be an important part of everyone's future. Equally important to these ladies was to fly the race as a team. As much as each desired to win, they helped each other throughout, with the hope that all would finish the race.

These young women had learned that if they wanted something badly enough, and worked hard enough, they could conquer all odds. What they accomplished and the courage it took to fly these small, fragile airplanes in this race was remarkable. And in doing so, they opened the first of many doors to allow today's women to fly as pilots for airlines, corporations, the military, and command space shuttles. It's been a long, hard fight.

My mother, Louise Thaden, was one of the pilots in this "Powder Puff Derby." She was an ordinary young girl from Arkansas when she

fell in love with the sheer joy of flying. Just as in doing anything we love to do, being in the air made her spirits soar, and she dared to dream of soaring on the wings of flight.

By working hard and never giving up, she met the challenges she faced every day in her aviation career, and lived her dreams. She earned her right to be called one of the greatest pilots of her day and a legendary pioneer of aviation's "Golden Age."

Throughout her lifetime, my mother always found new doors to open and new challenges to meet. She proved that regardless of gender, race, or age, that wise saying is true for us all: "We Can Because We Think We Can."

Louise Thaden stands with daughter Pat in front of their plane en route to a 1951 ceremony renaming the Bentonville, Arkansas, airport as "The Louise M. Thaden Field."

· · · · · · ·

Her greatest wish for you would be that you dream big, and that you live your dreams just as she did.

Pat Thaden Webb

Prologue

"Racing, of course, is not the safest sort of flying."
· · · · · · ·

AMELIA EARHART

Monday evening, August 19, 1929: Seventeen young women wearing crumpled clothes and forced smiles sit at a banquet table in the ballroom of the glamorous new Westward Ho Hotel in downtown Phoenix. They impatiently chew on their fried chicken and listen to speeches about the newly established Arizona chapter of the Exchange Club, a civic association with branches all over the country and the sponsor of their race. They are bone tired after hours of flying over the Arizona desert, most of them in open-cockpit planes, with the sun burning down, the wind blowing sand in their faces, and the heat creating a haze that makes it hard to see. The roar of the engines is still ringing in their ears.

The women are pilots, female pioneers in the exciting new field of aviation, and they would much rather be doing other things right now.

· · · · · · ·

A light-hearted pose during the first overnight stop in San Bernardino. Back row includes (far left) Thea Rasche, and (far right) Ruth Elder and Edith Foltz. Front row, sitting on car (left to right): Vera Dawn Walker and Louise Thaden.

They are competing against each other in a cross-country race that has been jokingly dubbed "The Powder Puff Derby" because of the fact that all the pilots are women. But this contest is no joke. It is a grueling, nine-day competition in which these women must fly 2,800 miles over deserts, mountains, and plains in extreme heat with nothing but a compass and some road maps to help them find their way. The women's planes need servicing and refueling, and they feel uneasy about leaving their planes unguarded. There have been warnings of sabotage—people deliberately tampering with the planes to damage them and affect the outcome of the race—even before the contest

Two hours before the race, Claire Fahy had a close call while being flown around the airfield by Wiley Post. A sudden wind caused Wiley to almost lose control of the plane and crash.

· · · · · · ·

began. Now, as they smile and nod their heads and pretend to listen to the long speeches, they worry. And they are exhausted! Even if they were to leave the banquet being held in their honor right this minute and not return to the airfield to check on their planes, they would still only get a few hours of sleep before continuing the race. They have to be up and ready to fly at dawn.

It is only day two of the race and already so many things have gone wrong!

There should have been 20 of them.

Claire Fahy, who was being followed by a plane piloted by her record-breaking aviator husband, was the first to quit. Earlier that day she'd made a forced landing in Calexico, California, on the border with Mexico, claiming foul play and spreading more worry about sabotage. Somebody, she charged, had deliberately poured acid over her plane's wire wing braces!

Nineteen-year-old Mary Haizlip, who, like Claire, was taught to fly by an aviator husband, was a day late getting started. She had to wait for the delivery of a new plane, after having a host of mechanical troubles with her first one. Then she got lost across the border on the Mexican side of the Baja Peninsula. She now has to get clearance from the Mexican authorities before they let her fly back to the United States to join the other women in the race.

But, most worrisome of all, a flyer is missing!

Marvel Crosson is among the most experienced of the women flyers in this race. Everyone likes her, with her direct, friendly manner and bright smile. Her yellow Travel Air plane, inscribed with the bold number 1, has yet to show up. Marvel had troubles even before the race began, and she ordered a new engine to be delivered to her in Phoenix, the second overnight stop on the race. Now troubling rumors are circulating at the banquet. Several ranchers are said to have seen a plane spinning high up in the air above the desert before plunging into a grove of cottonwood trees.

Was it Marvel?

Many thought she had a good shot at winning this race. Less than two months before the race, she had broken the previous women's

Mary Haizlip, only 19 at the time of the race, had enrolled in a flying school and ended up marrying her instructor, a former World War I flying ace.

· · · · · · ·

record for altitude, her plane reaching an amazing 23,996 feet, more than three-quarters of the height of the world's highest peak, Mount Everest. At age 25, Marvel has already been flying for years. Together with her brother Joe, they run a private airplane company and fly people around the rugged mountains and wilderness of Alaska. Joe tested Marvel's brand new Travel Air plane after he picked it up fresh from the factory. He got it up to a speed of 168 miles an hour, making it quite likely the fastest plane to enter the race.

And Marvel wasn't one to take unnecessary chances. She flew a practice run along the route she would take on the race.

Where is Marvel?

· · · · · · ·

By the time they got to Douglas, Arizona, their next overnight stop, they knew the dreadful answer to that question.

The body of Marvel Crosson was found, some distance away from the wreck of her "Number One" plane. It looked as if the plane developed mechanical trouble, and she may have tried to bail out. Her bones were broken; and searchers saw her parachute tangled around her. She may have tried to open her parachute, but by the time she pulled the rip cord, it was too late.

The outcry is immediate. "STOP THE RACE" screams a newspaper headline in El Paso, Texas, one of their next stops. "Airplane Races Too Hazardous an Adventure for Women Pilots," says an editorial in the *New York American*. The Santa Monica sponsor of the race calls for an immediate halt, saying the girls' planes are not being properly guarded during their overnight stays and there may have been tampering, even sabotage.

But the women are united in their refusal. "We wish officially to

· · · · · ·

Marvel Crosson flew a brand-new Travel Air with one of the newest engines. When Marvel's brother Joe tested the plane, it went up to 168 miles an hour, making it quite possibly the fastest plane in the race.

thumb our collective nose" at the idea of stopping mid-race, the race's manager tells reporters.

Determined, the women flyers insist on continuing.

On with the race!

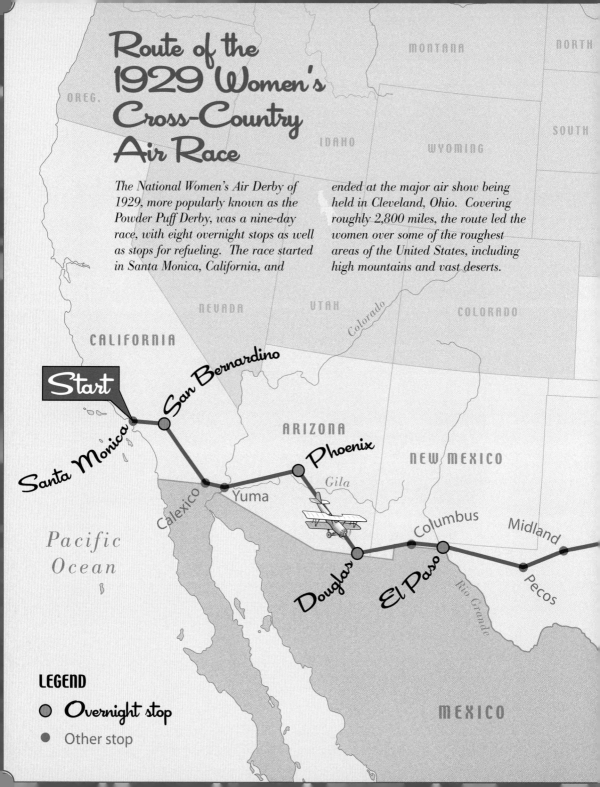

Route of the 1929 Women's Cross-Country Air Race

The National Women's Air Derby of 1929, more popularly known as the Powder Puff Derby, was a nine-day race, with eight overnight stops as well as stops for refueling. The race started in Santa Monica, California, and ended at the major air show being held in Cleveland, Ohio. Covering roughly 2,800 miles, the route led the women over some of the roughest areas of the United States, including high mountains and vast deserts.

LEGEND

● Overnight stop

● Other stop

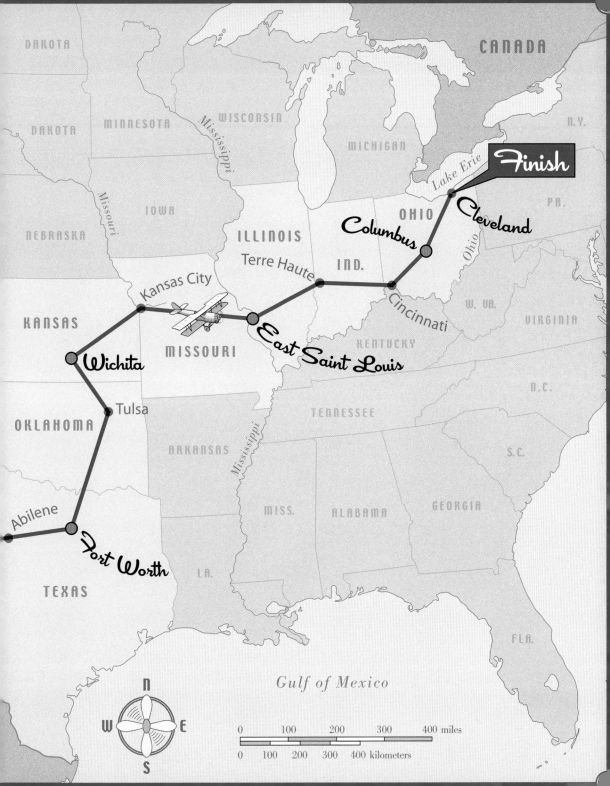

CHAPTER 1

The "Roaring" Twenties

"The times are glum and getting glummer, still we have fun!"

FROM A POPULAR SONG OF THE 1920S

Sometimes it is fun to think of historical periods as if they were individual people, each with his or her own particular style and personality. If you did that for the United States in the 1920s, the period between the two world wars, you might think of a brash energetic young person: fit and full of fun and roaring off to new places and trying new things. This was also the period during which the average American could finally afford one of those newfangled automobiles with their roaring engines. So it should come as no surprise that this period of history is called "The Roaring Twenties."

The First World War was horrible, as all wars are, but the United States had not entered the fray until 1917, jumping in with all its industrial and economic strength and playing a critical role in achieving an Allied victory. Americans were feeling pretty good about themselves.

The "flappers" had a style quite different from young women of the previous generation: They cut their hair, flattened their chests, and showed as much leg as possible, especially while dancing the Charleston!

They had flexed their muscle in the international arena—and the results had been impressive.

Women, too, were feeling good about themselves. Their husbands and sons and sweethearts had gone off to war, and most of them had been lucky enough to come back in one piece. In the meantime, women had pitched in to help out. Some of them had found jobs in a marketplace that was much more welcoming to them than before the war. (After all, workers were scarce during wartime!) For the first time in U.S. history, some women had officially enlisted in the military. In the Navy and Marine Corps they were known as "yeomanettes" or "Marinettes." Other adventurous women volunteered as Red Cross nurses or nurses' aides both at home and abroad. One of them was Amelia Earhart, future Powder Puff Derby entrant, who temporarily dropped her college studies to work at a Canadian military hospital where thousands of soldiers were being treated for serious war-related ailments, including poison gas burns; small pieces of bomb, mine, or shell in the lungs; and tuberculosis. Other young women came to Washington, D.C., to support the war effort in government jobs, or worked in other towns in defense or defense-related factory work.

In 1919, in the flush of victory and in a generous mood, thankful to all the women who helped in the war effort, Congress passed the 19th Amendment to the United States Constitution allowing women the right to vote. By the summer of 1920, all the states had ratified the amendment. In a country founded on the proposition that "all men are created equal," women were now included as well. After decades of struggle, women finally were able to vote for their government representatives.

In the world of fashion, too, things were changing. Holding down jobs and living independently influenced the way women dressed and

THE
EXCHANGITE

OCTOBER
1929

The fashionable woman of the 1920s rejected the sweet, conventional, girl-next-door image. The "flapper" wanted to be bold, sophisticated, and cause a flap!

· · · · · · ·

even the way they moved. They were no longer willing to put up with the difficulty of walking in long narrow skirts with hems that would get muddied in the streets, or being unable to breathe in stifling corsets, or spending hours caring for and styling their long hair. It was so much easier to move around wearing shorter skirts and comfortable under-clothing, and to have one's hair cropped short (or "bobbed" as they called it) in a man's barber shop.

Many people–including women–flaunted Prohibition laws by carrying hidden flasks, brewing home-made alcohol, and socializing at secret nightclubs called "speakeasies" where illegal drinks were served.

· · · · · · ·

And did those skirts ever shorten! In 1919, hemlines were still at the ankle. By 1927 they were above the knee!

Once these women were moving around more freely and comfortably, is it any wonder that their behavior loosened up as well?

Many young women went to clubs at night wearing their short skirts and dancing till all hours to the new, jazzier kind of music. They were called "flappers" because one of the dances they popularized included a birdlike flapping of the arms combined with a lively

"Charleston" step. These young women were willing, even eager, to try new things, unafraid of causing "a flap" or shocking the older, more tradition-bound generation.

But let us add something darker to this symbolic portrait of a brash young person in a hurry: This person was willing to cheat or lie in order to come out ahead. The 1920s was a period during which an ambitious social experiment called "Prohibition" was tried—and failed. Starting in January 1920, U.S. law prohibited the making, transporting, and selling of alcohol. Yet many people went out to socialize at "speakeasies," secret nightclubs where illegal alcohol was served and women were welcomed; doctors prescribed "medicinal" liquor; and people began making up their own homemade brews, some of them with unsafe ingredients. Many whiskey distributors moved large amounts of their supply offshore to islands like the Bahamas, then "bootleggers" smuggled the liquor into the country. Al Capone and other gangsters made enormous profits distributing and selling the illegal drinks. There were many corrupt politicians and policemen willing to look the other way while these illegal activities were going on. This attitude spilled into the sports arena as well—and, as we will see in a later chapter, even affected air races.

Aside from a new freedom for women, the First World War also ushered in a tremendous popular interest in flying. The automobile had been around since the beginning of the century, but the airplane was a newer, faster, and more exciting mode of transportation.

The First World War was fought in the skies as well as the traditional combat on land and on the seas. There were "dogfights" in the air: combat between airplanes flown by opposing pilots. Soon the airplanes were armed with machine guns and eventually bombs, so pilots could not only attack each other but also hit targets on the ground.

The war stimulated advances in flying as governments poured money and resources into the development of new and better airplanes that were not only faster but could climb higher and carry heavier loads for longer periods of time.

After the war, with the disbanding of the armies and a drastic reduction of the air services, the government was left with many surplus airplanes. They were sold for moderate prices (several hundred dollars) and for the first time, people did not have to be extremely rich to own and fly an airplane (though it was still far from inexpensive to maintain one). There were also lots of former war pilots who were only too happy to make money by teaching people how to fly in the newly established flying schools.

Although many Americans were fascinated by this new form of transportation, there was still a widespread belief that flying was a dangerous, even foolhardy thing to do. Early pilots were testing the limits of aviation in planes that were often made of light wood and fairly flimsy in construction, yet carrying heavy water-cooled engines that could quickly overheat or malfunction. The controls and navigational aids used to guide their flights were still primitive. So it is not surprising that there were many crashes, each reported in horrifying detail in the newspapers. Most Americans, while fascinated, preferred to be spectators and leave the flying to professional pilots.

The first air shows had to be performed in large, open farmers' fields where there was lots of empty space. Pilots, to thrill the crowd, would often fly dangerously low over the farmers' barns, which led to the term "barnstorming." To attract a big crowd and put on a good show, these early pilots felt they had to do extraordinary things. They would fly fast and high, performing loops, rolls, and steep dives to entertain their audience. For added thrills, they would sometimes have a performer with them who would carry out acrobatic tricks such as walking, dancing, or balancing on the wings; or hang by their legs from the landing gear, or by an arm from a bar suspended from the wing tip. They called these daredevils, often attractive young women, "wing walkers." One of them was young Phoebe Omlie, before her marriage named Phoebe Fairgrave, a future pilot in the Powder Puff Derby. Phoebe's routine was to walk on the wings of an airplane and then leap down in a parachute. By the time she was 20, she had her own show called "The Phoebe Fairgrave Flying Circus."

· · · · · · ·

Stunt flyer Lillian Boyer hangs from the wing of a biplane in midair. Having attractive women perform dangerous air stunts was one way to draw crowds to an air show, but it was definitely not the safest way to earn a living!

During the 1920s, daredevil pilots and stunt performers would try almost anything. Here Gladys Roy (top) and Ivan Unger pretend to enjoy a game of tennis several thousand feet up.

. . . .

Sometimes the best part of the show would be when the pilot finished his fancy tricks, parked his plane in the field, and then offered the braver spectators the chance to pay a few dollars to go up in the two-seater airplane with him. Some of these gutsy customers were

· · · · · · ·

Here Charles Lindbergh is seen starting his engine during his appearance
at the air show in Cleveland. After Lindbergh's 1927 solo flight across the
Atlantic Ocean, he became a national hero and ignited great interest in aviation.

young women who got their first taste of flying that way. Once they were in the air, they saw the breathtaking view from up high, and they felt the rush of the wind and the soaring sensation of flying. Was it any wonder that some of them wanted to pilot their own planes? Soon a new word was in use—"aviatrix"—meaning "woman flyer."

As pilots of both genders tested the limits of this new technology, there was a rush to be the first: First to cross the country in a plane, first to cross the English Channel in a plane, first to cross the ocean in a plane, and so on. There were financial rewards to spur them on. Raymond Orteig, the owner of some New York hotels, offered $25,000 to the first person to fly solo from New York to Paris—clear across the Atlantic Ocean—in one non-stop airplane ride. Orteig made that offer back in 1919, but it was not until May 1927 that young Charles Lindbergh—more popularly known as "Lucky Lindy"—won the prize and became a national hero.

After her widely publicized attempt to cross the Atlantic, Ruth Elder starred in several movies, including Moran of the Marines, *with Richard Dix and Jean Harlow, and* Winged Horsemen *with Hoot Gibson.*

· · · · · · ·

The two trends—the move toward equality for women and the interest in aviation—hit at about the same time and produced a generation of daring, competitive aviatrixes. Lindbergh may have been the first man to fly solo nonstop from the United States to Europe, but now there was competition to be the first woman. Ruth Elder, a glamour girl originally from Florida, who would later race in the Powder Puff Derby, attempted it only a few months after Lindbergh. The weather was poor, but Ruth, in a hurry to be the first woman to cross, made a go at it anyhow with her male co-pilot George Haldeman, in a plane christened the "American Girl." They crash-landed in the Atlantic Ocean and were fished out of the sea by a passing Dutch freighter. As their damaged plane was being hauled up on deck, it burst into flames.

Other women competed to be the first woman to cross the Atlantic, but it was Amelia Earhart who was the first to make it safely across. The fact that Amelia was only a passenger and neither piloted nor navigated the plane did little to dampen the public acclaim she received, in both Europe as well as in the United States. Amelia's resemblance to the aviator hero, Charles Lindbergh, probably added to her popularity. Both of them were tall, slim, and fair-haired, with ready grins. In personalities, they both were outwardly friendly, casual, and modest, in refreshing contrast to their celebrity status. The press dubbed Amelia "Lady Lindy," linking her with Lindbergh in the public mind.

After Amelia's historic flight, there were a series of attempts by other women pilots to join the list of firsts, highest, fastest, but most especially to set what they called "endurance" records for the longest time up in a plane. These competitions were among women only; they did not even try to compete with the records of men. Most, but not all, of them were to be future entrants in the Powder Puff Derby: Bobbi Trout, who stayed up in her plane for 12 hours, 11 minutes on January 2, 1929; teenage pilot Elinor Smith who stayed aloft for 13 hours, 16 minutes in an open cockpit biplane on January 31; and Louise Thaden, who made it to 22 hours, 3 minutes on March 16-17. Louise Thaden also made a record for the highest altitude, reaching 20,260 feet on December 7, 1928, until she was bested by Marvel Crosson who on May 28, 1929, reached just short of 24,000 feet above Los Angeles.

After the war, many of the early women pilots discovered a new way to make a living—as demonstrators of commercial aircraft. It was a lot safer than performing those dangerous tricks in an airplane, and it paid well enough to help support their still-expensive hobby. U.S. plane manufacturers needed to show flying was a safe and convenient mode of transportation, suitable for the busy businessman, not just for performers in air shows. What better way to illustrate the safety of aviation than to use women pilots as the sales persons and demonstrators? Why, this plane is so safe and easy to operate that even a woman can pilot it! Among

An ardent feminist, Amelia Earhart sought to downplay her feminine side. She frequently chose to wear trousers and boyish jackets, and sported a short, tousled hairstyle.

· · · · · · ·

these demonstration pilots were Louise Thaden, Bobbi Trout, and Ruth Nichols, all of whom would participate in the Powder Puff Derby. Soon there was a whole generation of women flyers who made their living and gained valuable flying experience working for airplane manufacturers. These women were just itching to show what they could do in these new planes, and they watched enviously as male pilots earned fame and fortune in air races.

CHAPTER 2

The Rules of the Race

"This race is going to show people that we women can fly."
. . . .
RUTH ELDER

A major air show, including air races, was scheduled to be held August 24 to September 2, 1929, in Cleveland, Ohio. Air shows had been held since 1920, mainly to stimulate public interest in aviation. Promoters of flying and civic boosters in Cleveland hoped that the 1929 show would be the biggest and best one yet. There would be pilots competing for trophies by racing their planes around closed courses marked by pylons. There would be men's cross-country races starting from Los Angeles, Miami, and Toronto, all timed to reach Cleveland on different days of the show. There would be floats and marching bands, Goodyear blimps, aerial acrobatic shows, fireworks, displays of all the latest models of airplanes, the release of 5,000 pigeons, and even an appearance by the aviation hero Charles Lindbergh himself.

. . . .

The women pilots were racing from Santa Monica to Cleveland, the site of the 1929 air show. Cleveland city officials were determined to make it the aviation event of the decade. Three hundred thousand people turned out for opening day.

Clifford Henderson (left) talks to Major Georges Thenault, air attaché at the French Embassy, at the 1929 National Air Races. Henderson was managing director of all the races, including the Women's National Air Derby.

· · · · · · ·

But even more excitement was generated when the National Exchange Club decided to sponsor a Women's National Air Derby. Women would get the chance to race cross-country to the air show, too.

Cliff Henderson, organizer of the men's races, agreed to manage the event along with an all-male committee. They all thought it a grand idea, until they got down to the specifics. They soon learned that they had underestimated the seriousness of women flyers. To begin with, the committee did not really want it to be a cross-country race. They feared that flying over the mountains would be far too dangerous for women. Perhaps the ladies should start in Omaha, they suggested.

Amelia Earhart, the most famous of the women flyers and eager to prove to the public that she was now a skilled pilot, not just a pretty passenger, was outraged. She insisted the race would have to start in California if it were to be billed as a truly cross-country race.

Then the committee suggested that if the women insisted on flying cross-country, they might need the assistance of men who were

· · · · · · ·

An announcement in the Daily Dispatch *of Douglas, Arizona, invites people to watch the women land on the third day of the race. Although it advertised 25 flyers in the race, five of these women dropped out before the race began.*

'SWEETHEARTS OF THE AIR'

WOMEN'S NATIONAL AIR DERBY

Santa Monica, California, to Cleveland, Ohio.

25 Entrants In All!

INCLUDING
MISS RUTH ELDER—LADY MARY HEATH—GLADYS
O'DONNELL—AMELIA EARHART—BOBBY
TROUT—MARVEL CROSSON

ARRIVING AT THE

INTERNATIONAL AIRPORT
DOUGLAS, ARIZONA

Tuesday, August 20th, 10 A. M., and Leaving Wednesday, 6 A. M.

FLYING IN TWO CLASSES OF PLANES, FROM THE
SMALLEST TO HIGHEST POWERED MAKES.

The Biggest and Most Spectacular Air Event in the History of Arizona!

DON'T MISS IT!

Daily Dispatch Douglas, Arizona

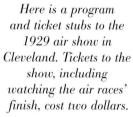

Here is a program
and ticket stubs to the
1929 air show in
Cleveland. Tickets to the
show, including
watching the air races'
finish, cost two dollars.

mechanics. What if their planes went down in the desert and the women didn't know how to repair them? After that suggestion, there was a sudden flurry of Hollywood starlets who wanted to enter the race. And a suspicion arose that those glamour girls were only seeking publicity—and that their male mechanics might do the actual flying!

Furious at the way things were shaping up, a group of women pilots, using the famous Amelia as their spokesperson, said they would boycott the race if they did not start in California and fly all the way to Cleveland. They also insisted that only women be allowed to enter the race. They sent a telegram of protest to both the National Air Races Committee and the committee organizing the women's event, with a statement to the press as well. Race manager Cliff Henderson persuaded the committee to agree to the women's demands. The rules were changed so that the women pilots would have to fly from California to Cleveland. If they had mechanics, the men would have to follow them in separate planes or by car and service the planes at the scheduled stops.

But the idea that a woman would be flying alone for long stretches of time over vast expanses of mountain and desert, especially in the

One popular souvenir from the air show and races was a gold chain bracelet with a winged medallion. The medallion could be engraved with one's name.

· · · · · · ·

dark with poor visibility, still concerned the race committee members. So they decided that women pilots would only fly during the daytime and they would land at regular intervals to eat, rest, and have their planes refueled. They would have someone record the pilots' starting and landing times and then add up the amount of time spent each day in the air. The winner of the race would be the pilot with the shortest flying time en route to Cleveland. The route began to shape up as a series of shorter-distance flights starting in Santa Monica, with eight overnight stops in San Bernardino, California; Phoenix, Arizona; Douglas, Arizona; Abilene, Texas; Fort Worth, Texas; Wichita, Kansas; East St. Louis, Illinois; and a final night in Columbus, Ohio, before the final victory lap into Cleveland. There were also to be some additional in-between stops for refueling, resting, and eating, and of course for more Exchange Club-sponsored social events.

Other rules were added to make an all-women cross-country race less frightening to the public, as well as to ensure the safety of

International pilots were licensed by the Federation Aeronautique Internationale (known as the F.A.I.). Thea Rasche had problems with her plane's license running out during the race.

· · · · · · ·

the pilots. There would be an attempt to keep the women flying together as much as possible, to prevent one woman from becoming totally isolated from the others while in the air. They hoped to accomplish this by having the last woman to fly in at the end of the day be the first one to take off in the morning. In addition, each woman had to wear a parachute strapped to her body while flying, so she could jump from the plane if there were serious mechanical troubles. At the time, parachutes were not standard equipment for pilots, and many scoffed at the idea of wearing one, saying they were for sissies. It was shortly after the Powder Puff Derby, in September 1929, that student flyer Fay Gillis had her picture in all the aviation magazines showing her smiling and holding up the parachute that had broken her fall and saved her life when her plane's tail broke off and the plane crashed.

Each woman was required to carry a gallon of water and enough food to survive for three days, in case she crashed in the desert. Amelia Earhart reported that she packed several cans of tomatoes and a can opener!

Finally, each woman was required to have a flying license from the Department of Commerce and the FAI (Federation Aeronautique Internationale)—and to have logged 100 hours flying solo, 25 of those hours long-distance (long distance defined as more than 40 miles from the starting point). Each entrant's plane also had to be licensed by the Department of Commerce.

In addition, the race committee decided to divide the race into two separate sections: one for the lighter planes with smaller engines, and one for the heavier planes with bigger engines. Unfortunately, that meant the prize money of $8,000 would have to be shared between the winners of the two divisions.

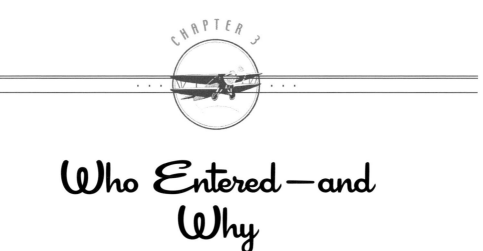

CHAPTER 3

Who Entered—and Why

"It looks like a Powder Puff Derby to me!"

. . . .

WILL ROGERS

The most famous entrant in the Powder Puff Derby, then as well as now, was Amelia Earhart. A basically modest and honest person, she was uncomfortable with all the celebrity treatment she received for being the first woman to cross the Atlantic. After all, she had been only a passenger and the real credit, she insisted, belonged to the pilot and the navigator. But the more she protested, the less people listened, so eventually she just resigned herself to all the public acclaim. Meanwhile, she became determined to cross the Atlantic again, but next time as the pilot. A solo crossing would make her more deserving of the fame she already had. Entering the first cross-country race for women would be the first of a series of tests she had set for herself that would enable her to develop the skills necessary to fulfill her goal of piloting across the Atlantic by herself. She was a

. . . .

Amelia Earhart became an international celebrity as the first woman to fly across the Atlantic. With publicist George Putnam's guidance, she made paid public appearances all over the country until she was able to buy her own plane.

woman in a hurry. She had just turned 31 on the day she signed up for the race, which made her older than most of the other women pilots.

Hovering by her side to prepare for this race was the handsome, sophisticated George Palmer Putnam, publisher-promoter who had taken Amelia on as his special project. He was the one who taught Amelia to smile with her lips closed to hide the gap between her front teeth. "G.P.," as he was nicknamed, was as ambitious as Amelia, probably even more so. He intended to make Amelia the most famous woman flyer in America. His feelings toward his number-one client were also becoming more personal. He felt a growing attraction to this slim young woman who looked so good in pants (still an unusual and daring style for women in those days). But he was already married to the daughter of a Pittsburgh millionaire, and he was the father of two sons. He would worry about his feelings toward Amelia after the race.

G.P. was not the only one trying to push romance from his mind. Just before the race, a Hollywood producer named Walter Camp, Jr. had proposed marriage to Ruth Elder and now she found herself faced with a serious distraction. She already had had two failed marriages and was unsure about marrying again so soon.

This race was not the first time Ruth Elder found herself competing against the formidable Amelia Earhart. They had competed to be the first woman to cross the Atlantic, and Amelia had won. Now they were competing again, and both were in the spotlight. One reason the cameras kept focusing on them was that both of these women were so attractive, but in entirely different ways. Whereas Amelia looked

· · · · · · ·

In her hometown of Lakeland, Florida, in 1927, Ruth Elder stands by the plane in which she learned to fly. She was then married to her second husband, Lyle Womach, who traveled with Commander Byrd to the South Pole.

"Pancho" Barnes' first name was Florence, but no one ever called her that.
She wore jodhpurs and her trademark beret throughout most of the race, and
was often mistaken for a man. She loved to fly, but most especially to fly fast.

wholesome in a casual but tailored sort of way, Ruth was a glamour girl. Nicknamed "Miss America of Aviation," she was a raven-haired beauty who played the leading female role in a Hollywood movie after her attempt to cross the Atlantic failed. Rumors spread that her failed attempt and subsequent rescue had just been a publicity stunt for her movie-star career. She was determined to end those rumors once and for all by competing solo in this race in her bright red "Swallow."

Now if Ruth Elder was a glamour girl, then Florence Barnes was the opposite. The feminine, old-fashioned sounding name of "Florence" did not suit her at all. Everyone called her "Pancho," a name she got while crewing on a boat smuggling guns into Mexico during the Mexican Revolution. She was known to curse like a sailor, ride fast horses as well as fast planes, and wear men's clothes. She smoked cigars (at a time when women were just beginning to smoke), lighting them with kitchen matches that she struck on the seat of her pants. During the race she wore jodhpurs (pants cut full through the hips and close-fitting from knee to ankle, worn when riding horses), high leather boots, and a beret. But no one ever doubted that she was a flyer, and a skilled one at that. She had done stunt flying for the movies and earned the respect of the toughest stunt men in the business when she organized them into their first union, which later became the powerful MPPA (Motion Picture Pilots Association).

Pancho was raised in the lap of luxury in Pasadena, California. The family fortune originally came from Pancho's famous grandfather, Thaddeus Lowe, the Civil War balloonist on the Union side, who used to go up in a balloon and from such heights spy on enemy camps. He studied engineering and gas technology, as well as wind currents, for his balloon flights, and later applied some of that research to invent a process for making ice (leading to refrigeration) and for manufacturing artificial gas for power needs. As a girl, Pancho often pulled bizarre practical jokes, such as the time at boarding school when her room-mate found her lying face down in a pool of red ink with a fake suicide note pinned to her blouse saying that she had killed herself! Pancho had been married off early to an Episcopalian minister in an unsuccessful attempt to tame her wild, adventurous spirit. After Pancho learned to fly, she liked to drown out her husband's sermons by flying low over his church on Sundays. Pancho thought flying in the first cross-country race for women would be a wonderful adventure.

Louise Thaden was a much more serious, reserved sort of person. A tough competitor, Louise went into the race having at one time or another achieved three different women's records: fastest speed, solo endurance (longest time up in an airplane), and highest altitude (until Marvel beat her). Though she loved the thrill of flying a race, she found all the social events and banquets that seemed to go along with being a woman racer exhausting. Tall and slender, with tousled hair and an "aviator's neck" (supposedly thin from all that swiveling around to see in different directions from the pilot's seat), her face would turn brown from sun exposure and she would lose ten pounds during the nine days of the race from a combination of hard flying, tense nerves, and monotonous banquet food.

During college, Louise switched from one major subject to another, until she dropped out and took a job in the sales department of the J.H. Turner Coal Company in Wichita, Kansas. But she still had trouble focusing. Whenever she had a break from work, she found herself drawn to the nearby Travel Air factory where they made and tested airplanes. Once she took a ride in one of their planes, she found her true calling in life. She was thrilled when she was offered a job working for Travel Air on the West Coast, with free flying lessons thrown in as a

· · · · · · ·

Goggles around her neck, holding her leather flying helmet, Louise Thaden stands in front of the Travel Air plane in which she made a record on March 16-17, 1929, for the longest solo endurance flight: over 22 hours up in the air.

bonus. She loved flying as well as competing, and was excited when she learned that women were finally being allowed to enter an air race. She enlisted the aid of her former boss Turner from the coal company, who was a director of Travel Air, to beg the head of Travel Air, Walter Beech, to make a plane for her to fly in the race. To get them to stop pressuring him, Beech agreed.

Marvel Crosson was a rover and an adventurer. Born in Indiana, she was raised on a ranch in Kansas and graduated from high school in Colorado. After graduation, she and her brother Joe moved to California, where they found parts of old Army surplus airplanes and rebuilt their own plane. The adventurous duo barnstormed for several years together before moving to Alaska, where they set up a commercial flying venture. She was considered one of the most experienced woman flyers, having logged hundreds of hours of flying time in one of the world's most rugged areas and having recently set the women's high-altitude record. She was the first woman to file the official entry papers for the race, which is how she got the number 1 on her plane.

Another woman considered to be an extremely skillful and experienced flyer, and therefore a possible race winner, was Ruth Nichols. Ruth had been flying for about 10 years by the time of the race. Raised in wealth and privilege, her first flight in 1919 was a high school graduation present. By 1923 she was the first woman licensed to pilot a "flying boat" (a plane that could take off and land on water). She went on to fly almost every type of aircraft developed, including glider planes with no engines, "airships" that were lighter than air, and, much later,

· · · · · · ·

Ruth Nichols was afraid of heights until her father got her a plane ride as a graduation present. The pilot performed acrobatic tricks in the air. Instead of making her scared, it made her laugh. She said she never feared heights again.

· · · · · · ·

Evelyn "Bobbi" Trout "bobbed" her hair in the 1920s and then kept
that easy, no-fuss hairstyle for many years after that. She was as gifted a
mechanic as she was a pilot, a rare combination in those days.

supersonic jets. To promote the fledgling Aviation Country Clubs that had started up around the country and to encourage more people to fly, Ruth flew to and landed in every state of the Union (48 back then). She was the first woman to do that.

Bobbi Trout was really named "Evelyn," but as with Florence Barnes, the name just didn't fit. Like the flapper girls, she "bobbed" her hair, a hairstyle she maintained throughout her life, and it is said that is where she got her nickname. She was not very feminine in the traditional sense, so the boyish nickname suited her. She was one of the only women in the race who did not need a mechanic. As a girl she knew so much about cars and motorcycles and their engines that she persuaded her parents to buy her a service station. But not long after she got her wish, she took her first ride in a Curtiss "Jenny" airplane at age 16 and from then on it was airplanes that claimed her attention. She held many records for altitude and endurance and was the first woman to fly at night.

These were just a few of the bold, colorful women who entered the 1929 air race. With the exception of Bobbi, the women described above entered the race in the heavyweight plane division. Among those entering with lighter-engine, smaller planes were former wing-walker Phoebie Omlie; Edith Foltz, the first woman to receive a pilot's license in the state of Oregon, who barnstormed across the Northwest with her husband right after they both learned to fly; Germany's first female stunt flyer Thea Rasche; and Australian Jessie "Chubbie" Keith-Miller, who became the first woman to fly from London, England, to Australia, when she took a trip with pilot Bill Lancaster, the year before the race. She started out as his passenger, but by the time she landed in Australia she knew how to pilot the plane! The fact that she had flown to Australia with a man who was not her husband scandalized as many as those who applauded her skill as a pilot.

CHAPTER 4

And They're Off!

DAY ONE: SUNDAY, AUGUST 18, 1929

· · · · · · ·

*Only 19 out of 20 pilots set off from Santa Monica, California,
to San Bernardino, California (68 miles)*

"I don't care what you guys write about their bravery, their skill, their sportsmanship, or their adaptability. What I'm gonna say is, 'Them women don't look good in pants.'"

That's what one male reporter at the race's start was overheard saying to the other men in the press tent. The first cross-country women's air race was attracting a lot of attention all right, but the attention was not always respectful!

Will Rogers was one of the most famous of the press covering the race. Will was a political and social commentator widely read and heard on the radio, as well as an entertainer of Cherokee Indian descent who performed Wild

· · · · · · ·

There was a flurry of last-minute preparations as the women readied for the race's start at Clover Field, Santa Monica. The planes lined up in two rows, with lighter airplanes in the front row. Many thousands came to see the women take off.

West rope tricks for audiences. He was known for his biting wit and sarcasm. For example, speaking of the election of then-President Calvin Coolidge, Will Rogers said: "He didn't do anything, but that's what people wanted done."

Will was also known to be deeply interested in the growing field of aviation. Helping him "cover" the event was his pal, the one-eyed pilot Wiley Post. Wiley had his left eye poked out while working with oil-drilling equipment in Oklahoma, but that didn't slow him down a bit.

Will Rogers and Wiley Post, friends and co-pilots, died together in 1935 when their plane crashed in Alaska on their round-the-world trip. Will Rogers is credited with being the first to call the race a "Powder Puff Derby," and the humorous name stuck.

Using the insurance money he received for the accident to buy his own plane and wearing a dashing eye patch, he went on to become a barnstormer. Both Will and Wiley were experienced long-distance pilots. They volunteered to fly the same route as the women in order to transport some of the race officials and even carry a load of the women's luggage in their plane, as well as comment on the action in the race.

Will Rogers and Wiley Post were there at the start of the race in Santa Monica, California, kicking the tires of the planes and making everyone laugh to relieve all the tension in the air. Twenty thousand people lined Clover Field, many of them swarming up an adjacent hill to get a better view. The airfield's nearness to Hollywood ensured that many celebrities attended, including cowboy movie star Hoot Gibson. The start-off was on a Sunday and the weather was fair, further guarantees of a good turnout. Up to the very last minute, bouquets of flowers were being delivered to the women pilots as they sat in their planes getting ready for takeoff.

Blanche Noyes received many bouquets of flowers during the race. Many fans in Cleveland, the site of the air show, which was the race destination, were rooting for their hometown girl to win. Before her marriage to an airmail pilot, she was an actress.

· · · · · · ·

The planes lined up in a double row: The front row was for the light planes and the second row for the heavier aircraft. At exactly 2 p.m., a pistol was fired in Cleveland, the end point of the race and the site of the air show. The shot was relayed by radio to the airfield in

The pistol shot signaling the start of the race was fired in Cleveland and then relayed by radio and carried over loudspeakers at Clover Field. Then the official starter at Clover Field signaled each woman when to take off by lowering a flag.
· · · · · · ·

· · · · · · ·

*Will Rogers called it a "Powder Puff Derby," but most likely Jessie Keith-Miller
was just wiping dirt off her face. Most of the women were flying in open-cockpit
planes at high speeds and were probably less than thrilled about being
photographed just after landing.*

Santa Monica where a red-and-white flag was dropped to signal each woman flyer, one every minute or two, to take off in the order of the number given to each plane. Phoebe Omlie was the first to take off among the lighter planes. Then, after all the lighter planes were sky-bound, Marvel Crosson was the first to take off piloting one of the heavier, big-engine planes. One by one, 19 planes took off.

There should have been 20, but Mary Haizlip, at 19 the youngest entrant in the race, was still nervously waiting for her plane to arrive. She would wind up starting a day late. But since the outcome of the race was determined by who finished the route in the least number of hours, she could still compete.

As Will Rogers watched the women flyers soar off into the blue sky, he said, probably in an attempt to break the tension with a light-hearted remark: "It looks like a Powder Puff Derby to me!" He was referring, of course, to the fact that many women wore makeup and frequently were seen in public patting powder on their faces. Feminists like Amelia Earhart were not amused, but the catchy name stuck.

After all the women pilots took off, a squadron of planes carrying race officials and the press followed after them. The first leg of the race was supposed to be a relatively easy 68-mile flight directly east to the first overnight stop in San Bernardino, California.

Amelia Earhart was the first to have trouble— one of many problems she would face in this race.

Amelia Earhart owned a second-hand Lockheed Vega. When Wiley Post declared it unfit to fly in, Amelia traded it in for another Vega. She had little time to practice flying her new plane before the race.

Amelia had not even crossed the border of the airfield when her plane turned. Soon it became obvious to everyone that she was returning, rather than racing to the east. She circled around and around, waiting for the rest of the flyers to finish taking off, as it would be difficult to land in all the smoke and dirt raised by so many airplanes. Clearly, something was wrong. A crew of mechanics waited anxiously as she cut her engine and steered her plane back to the takeoff point.

Looking at her control panel, Amelia saw that an electric switch had short-circuited. She decided to return now where she knew she had a safe place to land. She lost 14 minutes as she waited to have a new switch installed. Fourteen minutes . . . . bad, but not horrible, she thought, not nearly enough to keep her from winning the race.

But the late start made her eager to make up for lost time. Forty-three minutes later, when Amelia saw the huge letters on a rooftop spelling "San Bernardino," she zoomed down without waiting for the clouds of dust from the other women flyers and the arriving cars of spectators to clear. Without a good view of the runway, she landed with a big thud, and her plane bounced before rolling down the dirt runway, only to come to a halt just a few feet away from the spectators. They thought she was doing it to show off for them and they politely applauded, never realizing how close a call they had just had.

At this first stop in San Bernardino, Pancho Barnes was in the lead in the heavyweight division, Phoebe Omlie in the lighter aircraft.

After all the excitement and tension of the first day of the race, most of the women flyers just wanted to refuel, have their planes serviced and checked, and call it a day. But their San Bernardino hosts had big plans for the celebrity guests. They shuttled the women off in cars to a formal banquet being held in their honor, where they sat listening to speeches and watched *The Flying Fool*, a movie for

· · · · · · ·

Pancho Barnes had no problem turning her own propeller. She was used to servicing her own plane, lugging her own gear, and doing pretty much everything herself. She played hard, but she worked hard, too.

PATHE PRESENTS
WILLIAM
BOYD
IN
The Flying Fool

with
MARIE PREVOST
RUSSELL GLEASON
AND TOM O'BRIEN

Supervised by
WM. SISTROM
from original story by
ELLIOTT CLAWSON
Directed by
TAYLOR GARNETT

Pathe Picture

Pancho Barnes did stunt flying for Howard Hughes, the famous aviator/ moviemaker/millionaire, including special effects for flying sequences in Hughes' blockbuster movie, Hell's Angels. *For* The Flying Fool, *Pancho hired pilots for $100 a day, more than twice what Hughes usually paid them.*

· · · · · · ·

which Pancho had been technical director for the flying scenes.

At midnight the women were allowed to go back to their hotel, but they still could not get their well-deserved sleep. There was something important to be decided. Some of the women feared that the next stop on the race—Calexico—a town on the border between California and Mexico—did not have a landing strip big enough for the heavier aircraft. Pancho, with her experience organizing workers' unions of stunt flyers, led the protest. She quickly drafted a petition and got the women to sign it, saying that they refused to fly any further unless race officials agreed to let them land in Yuma, Arizona, where there was a bigger and safer airfield.

The local air race official in San Bernardino was reluctant to let the women change the course at the last minute. He wanted the approval of a high-ranking race official. Unfortunately, that official was back in Cleveland, and had left his phone off the hook before going to bed. The dispute continued for another two hours until someone in Cleveland personally visited the official's house, woke the man up, and worked out a compromise. The women could land in Yuma, but they still would have to fly over and be identified in the skies above Calexico.

Exhausted, the women flyers fell into bed to catch a few hours sleep before the race would continue at dawn.

CHAPTER 5

Sabotage?

DAY TWO: MONDAY, AUGUST 19, 1929

. . . .

From San Bernardino to Calexico, California, (220 miles), to Yuma (165 miles), to Phoenix, Arizona, (158 miles)–19 Pilots Remaining

E ven Pancho Barnes, among the most fearless of the pilots, was anxious about the possibility of sabotage. She worried that people might deliberately tamper with a plane to cre-ate mechanical trouble and put the plane or even the pilot out of the race. In later years in an interview, Pancho recalled that there was "a lot of heavy betting on these air races and [it was a] common practice for someone to tamper with the airplanes." Others feared that men wanting to show that women were inept pilots might tamper with the planes.

One of the women competitors particu-larly nervous about the possibility of sabotage

. . . .

Around the country, daily newspapers were filled with stories about the first women's cross-country air derby, from coverage of the accidents, collisions, mechanical failures, and sabotage to the aviation-related social events.

Thea Rasche, so fearless in her stunt flying back home in Germany, was filled with trepidation about the possibility of sabotage in her first U.S. cross-country race.

· · · · · · ·

during the race was Thea Rasche, Germany's first female stunt flyer and famous worldwide for her flying ability. The day before the cross-country race, she showed Louise Thaden an anonymous telegram she received that said: "Beware of sabotage." Louise took it seriously enough to tell Thea to show it to the race manager who calmly told her not to worry about it. But Thea continued to worry, especially the next day when she found garbage, including scraps of fiber and rubber, in her gas tank. There was enough to clog up her carburetor and force her down near Holtville, California. She informed the press that because of the sabotage, she was no longer trying to win the race. She would just have her plane fixed and then fly to Cleveland to compete in the closed- course racing events. She also publicly told reporters about the threatening telegram she had earlier shown to Louise.

Additional peculiar incidents made some of the other women worry about sabotage, too, or, at the very least, to question the competence of the men servicing their airplanes. When Ruth Elder was about to start out the second day from San Bernardino, on a routine pre-flight check she discovered that the mechanics had put oil instead of gasoline in her plane's gas tank. "Those guys are either terminally stupid or brain-dead," she said to the other flyers, furious.

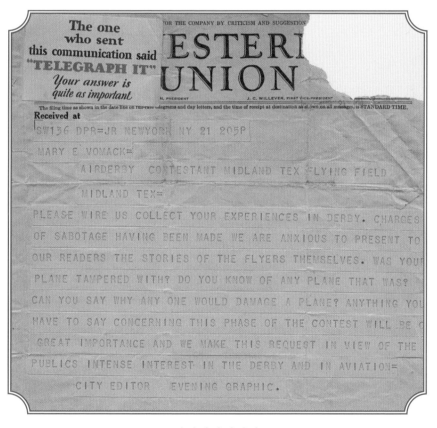

The one who sent this communication said "TELEGRAPH IT" *Your answer is quite as important*

FOR THE COMPANY BY CRITICISM AND SUGGESTION

WESTERN UNION

N. PRESIDENT   J. C. WILLEVER, FIRST VICE-PRESIDENT

The filing time as shown in the date line on full-rate telegrams and day letters, and the time of receipt at destination as shown on all messages, is STANDARD TIME.

Received at

SW136 DPR=JR NEWYORK NY 21 205P

MARY E VOMACK=

AIRDERBY CONTESTANT MIDLAND TEX FLYING FIELD

MIDLAND TEX=

PLEASE WIRE US COLLECT YOUR EXPERIENCES IN DERBY. CHARGES OF SABOTAGE HAVING BEEN MADE WE ARE ANXIOUS TO PRESENT TO OUR READERS THE STORIES OF THE FLYERS THEMSELVES. WAS YOUR PLANE TAMPERED WITH? DO YOU KNOW OF ANY PLANE THAT WAS? CAN YOU SAY WHY ANY ONE WOULD DAMAGE A PLANE? ANYTHING YOU HAVE TO SAY CONCERNING THIS PHASE OF THE CONTEST WILL BE OF GREAT IMPORTANCE AND WE MAKE THIS REQUEST IN VIEW OF THE PUBLICS INTENSE INTEREST IN THE DERBY AND IN AVIATION=

CITY EDITOR   EVENING GRAPHIC.

· · · · · · ·

Early on, reporters were eager to have stories about sabotage. But after the official investigation in San Bernardino was dropped, there was little in the way of proof to support the allegations, and so the number of stories about sabotage tapered off.

· · · · · · ·

At a press conference in California, Claire Fahy pointed to where she believed her plane's wires had been deliberately weakened. Her famous test pilot husband agreed and insisted that she drop out of the race for her safety. They called for an immediate investigation into sabotage.

But worse was yet to come. One pilot, Claire Fahy, had to make a forced landing in Calexico. Her husband, Lieutenant Herbert Fahy, a Lockheed Aircraft Company test pilot who was flying closely behind her, landed there, too; inspected the plane; and announced that someone had deliberately weakened her flying wires. These were the wires in a biplane that connected the upper wing to the lower wing and helped hold the plane together. Because she was flying in an open cockpit, Claire could hear the "twang" when the wires popped away from the plane. When she saw them dangling from her plane, she decided to make an emergency landing.

At a hastily called press conference, a clearly agitated Claire said that at her husband's urging she was dropping out of the race and demanded an inquiry be made into sabotage of the first cross-country women's air race. Flashbulbs popped at the image of the lovely female pilot, goggles pushed above her face, holding up her plane's wires and charging sabotage. Later, after the race, she said:

"I am convinced the wires had been tampered with . . . . I brought the wires back with me, and they [factory employees] say they never have seen a natural break similar to them."

Then when Marvel's plane went down near Yuma, there was even more talk about possible sabotage; though cooler heads remembered that Marvel had talked about engine trouble even before the race.

After the Fahys' charges, an investigation into possible sabotage was requested by the derby committee of the San Bernardino Exchange Club. On August 21, San Bernardino's district attorney George H. Johnson summoned 16 witnesses to testify about what might have happened during that night while the women flyers were at the banquet and then sleeping at their hotel. A railroad official testified that he had seen only one watchman at the San Bernardino airfield that night, hardly enough to guard so many planes. Other witnesses included the manager of Union Oil Company, who testified that none of his employees who serviced some of the planes had tampered with them; and officials of the derby and aviation experts who said they thought the mechanical problems probably were a combination of poor inspection and servicing, and a lack of adequate protection from curious visitors to the airfields. Claire Fahy's husband was called as a key witness, but for some reason refused to attend. Therefore, the hearings ended and the investigation was closed.

Meanwhile, the race continued, but the fear of sabotage lingered. As a result of the San Bernardino inquiry, the U.S. Army put armed guards around each of the women's planes for the next couple of night stops at Douglas, Arizona, and at El Paso, Texas.

People weren't only concerned about sabotage done to deliberately force someone out of the race. There was also the danger from a curious public. Jesse Keith-Miller, the Australian pilot nicknamed "Chubby" (which she wasn't), told a reporter in Phoenix that she hardly slept all night because she was so worried about whether she should be out guarding her plane. When she had returned to the airfield after the banquet in downtown Phoenix, she found "every switch and throttle on my plane—gas, ignition, primer, everything—turned on by inquisitive persons who climbed in and out of the planes at will with no one to stop them." This made her nervous that someone might accidentally damage her plane while playing around with the controls. Amelia Earhart said that at one stop she saw people jump onto her plane, walk the wings, and poke pencils or even umbrellas through the fabric-covered plane wings, as if testing to see what kind of material they were made of.

Pancho Barnes later recalled, "[We] . . . would put our planes in a circle like the old-fashioned ring of wagons [pioneers' covered wagons protecting themselves against Indian attacks], wing-tip to wing-tip, with our noses pointed toward the center. And then we'd hire two guards, one on the inside of the circle and [one] on the outside."

Bobbi Trout told a reporter in Yuma that although she had completely filled her gas tank the night before, she had to make an emergency landing due to an empty fuel tank. She believed that her fuel tank had been deliberately drained the night before. Forced to land in a plowed field in Mexico, her Golden Eagle cartwheeled on the furrows, causing damage to her entire plane. With the help of some locals, she had her plane towed over to Yuma where the plane was basically rebuilt. By the time her plane was flyable, she was three days behind the other women. She would continue in the race to Cleveland, but she knew she could not possibly win.

In a rare break during the race, Louise Thaden, in leather flying jacket, goggles, and scarf, sits by Gladys O'Donnell, wearing white flight suit, on a car's running board.

· · · · · · ·

A worried Louise Thaden asked the head of Travel Air, the company that had supplied her plane, to send one of their mechanics as soon as possible to join her at one of the stops along the race. When the mechanic inspected her plane at Abilene, Texas, and again at East St. Louis, Illinois, he found that someone had deliberately harmed a part in her engine. At Columbus, the all-important second-to-last stop before the race was to end in Cleveland, her mechanic said he was going to sleep next to her plane all night to ensure that no one tampered with it.

CHAPTER 6

Tragedy on Day Three

DAY THREE: TUESDAY, AUGUST 20, 1929

Phoenix to Douglas, Arizona (208 miles)—18 pilots remaining

According to Louise Thaden, the flyers were not officially told about what had happened to the popular Marvel Crosson until they were out of Arizona. Perhaps the race manager did not want to upset them while they were flying one of the most dangerous parts of the race. The course over Arizona ran over vast, wild desert where temperatures were more than 120 degrees, there was heat-induced turbulence and distortion in the air, and there were few if any landmarks to guide the pilots.

The desert sand not only made it hard to see but to land, too. While landing in Yuma,

As teenagers, Marvel Crosson and her brother Joe built their own plane using discarded and surplus plane parts. They barnstormed together in California before moving on to Alaska, where they ran a commercial air service.

A few planes like Marvel Crosson's brand-new Travel Air had closed cabins, but many of the women flew in open-cockpit planes. Controls and navigational equipment were relatively primitive.

. . . .

Arizona, Amelia's plane struck a big pile of sand and tipped over, its nose stuck in the sand like an ostrich. Repairs had to be made. The other women, normally so competitive, felt sorry for Amelia and voted to give her an extra one and a half hours without penalty while her propeller was fixed.

Meanwhile, shocked and dismayed by the death of one of the most popular members of their group, the women wracked their brains, trying to figure out what had gone so horribly wrong. Some recalled Marvel talking about problems with the engine on her brand new plane. She had ordered a new engine from Los Angeles but had ignored some of the women's urgent advice for her to wait until it arrived. Instead, not wanting to slow down, she had ordered it sent on ahead of her to the stop at Phoenix.

Others remembered Marvel saying she was not feeling so well that day. There were theories that she had lost consciousness, or felt so nauseated that she had leaned over the edge of her open cockpit to throw up and fell out. Many of the women knew how sick one could get while flying. For example, Louise Thaden had felt light-headed and nauseated from the engine's fumes while flying to California for the start of the race. She therefore had a four inch pipe installed through which she could breathe fresh air. Perhaps Marvel had passed out from lack of oxygen?

One aviation inspector from the Department of Commerce later speculated that it was "that time of month" for Marvel and that was the reason she got ill and lost control of the plane. After the race, an

· · · · · · ·

This is a picture of Yuma County, the desolate desert area where Marvel's plane crashed. It took all night and the next morning before the search party found her body in a thicket of trees and mesquite near the Gila River.

article in *The Journal of Aviation Medicine* warned women flyers under no circumstances to fly around the time of their menstrual periods.

But when Marvel's body was found with the parachute partially opened, some believed she was alert and conscious rather than sick or passed out, and had tried to parachute out of her failing plane.

The truth is, we will never know what really happened to Marvel in those last moments of her life.

Finding Marvel's plane wreckage and body was difficult, even after daylight. A search party on horseback, led by the deputy sheriffs of the nearest town in Arizona, combed an area of 100 square miles filled with dense thickets and trees on the banks of the Gila River. The men had to get off their horses and crawl on their hands and knees through the thicket. Eventually, they found the wreckage—and 100 yards away they found the body of Marvel crushed against a boulder, her neck and both legs broken.

Marvel's body was carried from the bush by horseback, and then driven by car to the nearest town of Wellton, Arizona, where it was put on a train back to her family home in San Diego.

Blanche Noyes, Louise Thaden, Pancho Barnes, Opal Kunz, and Mary von Mack were all flying the same kind of plane as Marvel—Travel Airs—or planes with Travel Air engines. So now there was some anxiety about the safety of their planes, along with the fear of sabotage!

After Marvel's body was found, some of the newspapers and members of the public called for a halt to the race, asserting that flying, especially air racing, was far too dangerous for "the gentle sex." When wealthy oilman Erle P. Halliburton was quoted in the newspapers as saying that "women have conclusively proven that they cannot fly," the women flyers grew angry, and more determined than ever that they must finish the race.

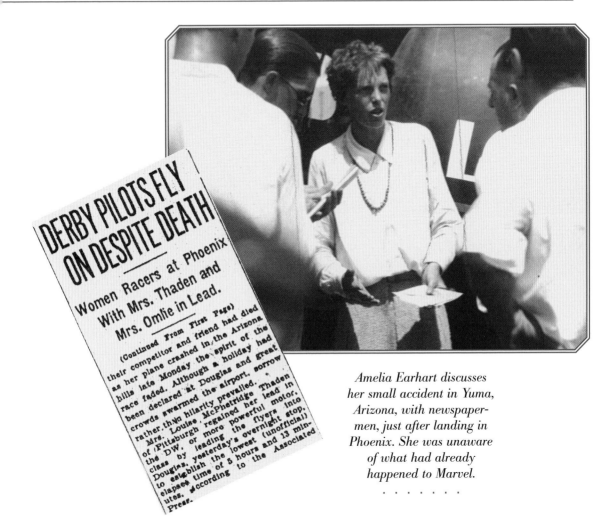

DERBY PILOTS FLY ON DESPITE DEATH

Women Racers at Phoenix With Mrs. Thaden and Mrs. Omlie in Lead.

(Continued From First Page)

their competitor and friend had died as her plane crashed in the Arizona hills late Monday the spirit of the race faded. Although a holiday had been declared at Douglas and great crowds swarmed the airport, sorrow rather than hilarity prevailed. Thaden of Pittsburgh regained her lead in the DW, or more powerful motor, class by leading the flyers into Douglas yesterday's overnight stop, to establish the lowest (unofficial) elapsed time of 5 hours and 13 minutes, according to the Associated Press.

Amelia Earhart discusses her small accident in Yuma, Arizona, with newspapermen, just after landing in Phoenix. She was unaware of what had already happened to Marvel.

· · · · · · ·

Louise Thaden later expressed the feeling of the whole group when she said that women had to be willing to risk their lives just as men had. "We women pilots were blazing a new trail. Each pioneering effort must bow to death. There never has been nor will there ever be progress without sacrifice of human life."

CHAPTER 7

Troubles in Texas

DAY FOUR: WEDNESDAY, AUGUST 21, 1929

Douglas, Arizona to Columbus, New Mexico, (188 miles),
Columbus to El Paso, Texas, (65 miles)

· · · · · · ·

DAY FIVE: THURSDAY, AUGUST 22, 1929

El Paso to Pecos (165 miles) to Midland (100 miles) to Abilene (14
miles) to Fort Worth, Texas, (138 miles)—16 pilots left in the race

I t was hard trying to get back into the competitive spirit of the race after the tragic death of Marvel Crosson. Gladys O'Donnell of California took it particularly hard. The bad news about Marvel came at about the same time as a telegram about the death in a plane crash of a young instructor at the flying school she and her husband ran back in California. Gladys cried hard, as did Louise. But Amelia spoke for the group when she told reporters that "It is now all the more necessary that we

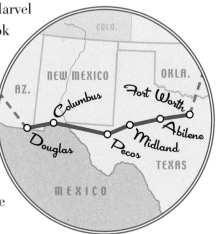

· · · · · · ·

Sandstorms in Texas made it hard for the women to land and then impossible to
take off when planned. Therefore, they had an unplanned overnight stop in El
Paso. The women were happy to have a night off from the usual banquets.

keep flying. We all feel terrible about Marvel's death but we know now that we have to finish."

So those who were crying dried their tears, and they all focused their minds for the hard days still ahead, as they would race across the vast state of Texas, which would include flying over the rugged Guadalupe Mountains and more desert.

The flyers also hit their first really bad weather in Texas. Coming into El Paso for what they thought would be only a fueling stop, they encountered such fierce winds and whirling sand that it was hard to land. Soon they were enveloped in a heavy sandstorm. They would have to stay in El Paso overnight.

In addition to the bad weather, overly enthusiastic spectators continued to be a big problem in this much publicized race. People were so excited to see beautiful young female pilots hop out of their flying machines—it was hard for them to believe their own eyes! They mobbed the airplanes as the women landed, stood dangerously close to the propellers or sat in cars parked too close to the runways, and even drove across the airfields just as planes were trying to land.

It was only a matter of time before an accident happened. As she zoomed into Pecos, Texas, only minutes behind Louise, Pancho Barnes' plane crashed into someone who was carelessly driving a car across the landing field. The field had looked clear as she approached, but Pancho had a blind spot from the bulky front of her Travel Air. Amazingly, both Pancho and the automobile driver walked away unhurt, but both vehicles were heavily damaged. It would take weeks to repair Pancho's airplane. It was put to a vote among the women flyers: Could they wait for Pancho to get a new plane and continue the race? No, they decided, Pancho was out for good.

Pancho was not the only one to have a close call in Texas. About

30 miles short of Pecos, Blanche Noyes smelled fire and saw smoke coming from her overhead baggage compartment! Frightened but willing herself to stay calm, Blanche made an emergency landing in the middle of the desert. She fought to pull out the fire extinguisher embedded in the floor of her plane. Using all of her strength, she finally yanked it out, taking half the plane's wood floor with it. Then the extinguisher didn't work! So she just opened up the luggage compartment, grabbed her burning suitcase with her bare hands, threw it out of the plane, and tossed sand on it to extinguish the flames.

Blanche then turned the propeller herself (usually a mechanic stood in front of the plane to do that while the pilot

Blanche Noyes, a hometown favorite from Cleveland, wearing her leather flying helmet, goggles, and flying jacket takes a moment to read correspondence during the race.

· · · · · · · ·

started the engine) and got her plane to take off, but without a proper airstrip the plane's bottom—fuselage, wings, and landing gear—got torn up by mesquite, the broad patches of thorny shrubs found in the deserts of the Southwest. Later, Louise would recall thinking as she watched Blanche land in Pecos that her plane "looked like a wounded

Before taking off from Douglas, Arizona, the planes are checked. Amelia Earhart's is in the foreground, the official derby plane next to it. Airplane engines were covered by tarps to protect them from dust.

. . . .

duck with a broken wing and badly crippled legs." Louise screamed for the crowd to get back from the field and called for fire extinguishers and an ambulance. But Blanche landed just fine, first on her right wheel that was still intact, then gently touching down with her broken left wheel.

Louise ran toward Blanche to see if she was all right. Blanche, her face black and her hands scorched, burst into tears, as she told of her horrible ordeal. Louise later defended Blanche's "typically feminine reaction" of crying by saying that Blanche had done a "spectacularly efficient job," and anyone—men included—would need "some outlet for emotional and mental stress." In Pecos, a welder helped her piece together her landing gear and she patched up her plane fabric with tape. She hoped her plane would hold up until the stop in Wichita where the Travel Air factory was located if she needed spare parts.

How had the fire started? Blanche found a cigarette butt in the plane's luggage compartment and guessed that the man who had helped her stow away her bag had probably been smoking. Rather than being angry,

Australian "Chubby" Keith-Miller was known as the first woman to reach Australia by plane. She started the flight from London as a passenger, but wound up as co-pilot.

· · · · · · ·

Blanche counted her blessings. The flames had come perilously close to reaching her gas tank!

"Chubby" Miller from Australia also had a close call. Somewhere between El Paso and Abilene, at 1,500 feet up in the air, her plane got caught in a whirlwind, a miniature twister. Her plane flipped several times in the air and was losing altitude fast. She debated whether to try parachuting from the plane, but perhaps remembering what had happened to Marvel she decided to try to ride the storm out. A few hundred feet from the ground, she was able to break away from the whirlwind and continue the race.

Meanwhile another woman, a licensed commercial pilot named Margaret Perry from California, had some bad luck in Texas, too. She had felt feverish earlier in the race,

Margaret Perry of Beverly Hills, California, felt sick early in the race. She tried to ignore it, but was finally pulled from the race and hospitalized.

but had stoically tried to ignore it. She finally gave up in Fort Worth, Texas, so gravely ill that she was admitted to a hospital. She was later diagnosed with the deadly typhoid fever! While flying the previous month, she had made a forced landing in a remote island village in Mexico and probably contracted the virus there. Margaret did regain her health, but she was out of the race.

CHAPTER 8

"Please God, Let Them All Be Cows!"

DAY SIX: FRIDAY, AUGUST 23, 1929

Fort Worth, Texas, to Tulsa, Oklahoma, (253 miles) to Wichita, Kansas, (130 miles)–still 15 pilots hanging in

Aside from mechanical troubles, sickness, carelessness of spectators, and possible sabotage, the next biggest problem for the women was just plain getting lost. Remember that in those days there were no sophisticated computer-directed navigation tools like pilots have today. They had only road maps and a compass. So how did these women know which direction to fly in the shortest possible amount of time? One way to do it was to fly low enough to use the road maps, looking for landmarks, and whenever possible to follow the railroads, which usually led the straightest way out of towns. Of course flying

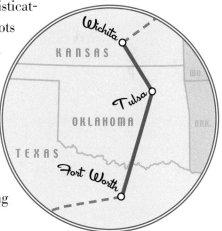

When a pilot had a mechanical problem or was lost, often the safest thing to do was to make an emergency landing in the nearest open field. Sometimes that field was occupied by someone who wasn't happy about uninvited company!

The women's planes were parked all in a row at the stop in Wichita, Kansas, home of Travel Air's factory. Louise Thaden's parents, as well as her sponsor, Walter Beech, came out to greet her there.

. . . .

Ruth Elder got lost several times during the race. The women had only a compass and some road maps, or they could try following the railroad tracks.

· · · · · · ·

low and fast was dangerous, as there were all kinds of potential hazards like telephone lines and trees.

Ruth Elder was one flyer who particularly had problems with getting lost. Despite the suspicion that Ruth was a publicity-seeking movie star rather than a serious flyer, she actually had quite a lot of experience flying solo— 300 hours by the time of the race. But once, when her plane hit air turbulence, she gripped her controls tightly with both hands and the strong wind blew all of her maps right out of her open cockpit. This was shortly after leaving Fort Worth, Texas. Ruth worried that with her bad sense of direction she would get lost. So she decided to land in the field below and ask for directions.

As she landed, Ruth realized it was not an empty field but a cow pasture. She thought of her bright red plane and prayed, "Please God, let them [all] be cows!" The last thing she needed was to have her plane charged by an enraged bull! Whether they were cows or bulls, they were curious about the strange thing that had landed among them and crowded close. Ruth chased them away, swinging her motor crank at them, before taking off again, deciding that she would continue without benefit of maps or directions. Although scary at the time, it was funny in hindsight and it later became one of the Powder Puff Derby contestants' favorite stories to tell.

Other flyers got lost when they were flying in the Southwest and wound up straying across the border into Mexico. That happened to Pancho Barnes when she followed the wrong railroad line. She realized her mistake when she heard the people around her yelling "*hola*" instead of "hello" and quickly revved up her engine and took off. The detour was just long enough to make her lose her lead in the race. Always one to poke fun at herself, Pancho at the next stop painted "MEXICO OR BUST" in big white letters across her plane.

Blanche Noyes got lost in a fog, and she, too, got lost in Mexico. She asked the people who crowded around her plane, "Where is the United States?" as she pointed at her map. No one understood her. When she saw a big group of men she feared might be bandits come galloping toward her on horseback, she got scared and took off in a big hurry.

Meanwhile, the glamorous Ruth had other things to worry about besides getting lost: like whether or not to accept the marriage proposal she had received just before the race began! By the time Ruth reached Wichita, she publicly confirmed what had already been rumored in the press: That at one of the overnight stops, she had phoned Walter Camp, Jr., a movie producer and former Yale football halfback, to say "yes."

CHAPTER 9

Troubles All the Way Through to the End

DAY SEVEN: SATURDAY, AUGUST 24, 1929

Wichita, Kansas, to Kansas City, Missouri, (175 miles) to East St. Louis, Illinois, (250 miles)

· · · · · · ·

DAY EIGHT: SUNDAY, AUGUST 25, 1929

East St. Louis, Illinois, to Terre Haute, Indiana, (158 miles) to Cincinnati Ohio, (158 miles) to Columbus, Ohio, (100 miles)—down to 14 pilots

· · · · · · ·

DAY NINE: MONDAY, AUGUST 26, 1929

Columbus, Ohio, to Cleveland, Ohio (120 miles)

The weather was unbearably hot at the race's beginning, often over 100 degrees Fahrenheit, but at least the skies were clear—except for the sandstorm in El Paso—until they hit the Midwest. Remember that most of these women, with a few exceptions such as Amelia Earhart, were flying in open-cockpit planes.

· · · · · · ·

People in the judges' stand and thousands of spectators, await the results of the national air races. Two men's races, in addition to the widely publicized women's race, were to finish in Cleveland where the big air show was taking place.

Imagine flying with a hard rain beating at your face and powerful winds blowing against you as you try to see to navigate your way to the next stop. Imagine rain flooding over your goggles and having to take them off to wipe them every couple of minutes. That kind of rain finally hit as they flew into Tulsa and then Wichita. Then in East St. Louis, there was a fog so heavy that the women could not see and had to wait for it to lift before taking off.

Due to mechanical troubles, Mary Haizlip started the race a day later than the others. She continued to have problems with her open cockpit American Eagle throughout the race.

· · · · · · ·

Meanwhile, young Mary Haizlip continued to be plagued by mechanical trouble. Instead of landing in East St. Louis, she had to make an emergency landing in the small town of Washington, Missouri, where she repaired a broken fuel line by herself. A farm boy attempted to crank the propeller for her, but she finally did that by herself, too, and zoomed off to try to catch up to the others.

German racer Thea Rasche almost got pulled from the race when the U.S. Department of Commerce informed race officials that her plane's license had expired on July 15th and they were going to ground her. But Director Frank Copeland talked the federal authorities in Washington, D.C., into letting Thea continue.

Bobbi Trout, though good at mechanics, began having more and more problems with her plane. Only a short hop from Cincinnati, where they were to make a stop, Bobbi had to make a dangerous emergency landing in a small fenced field near Greensburg, Indiana, and

further damaged her plane. The fence ripped a large hole in her "aileron" (the movable tab at the rear edge of an airplane wing which is used in banking into turns). She patched it up the best she could with a piece of tin can and some bailing wire, an engineer helped repair her engine, and she gamely continued in the race, knowing she was hopelessly far behind by now.

· · · · · · ·

Most of the women lined up for a group shot in East St. Louis on Sunday, August 25, while waiting for the morning fog to lift. From left to right: von Mach, Keith-Miller, O'Donnell, Rasche, Omlie, Thaden, Earhart, Noyes, Elder, and Walker.

Once the women reached Ohio, they knew they were in the home-stretch, with just three more stops in that big state: Cincinnati, Columbus, and then finally, the triumphant end of the race at the air show in Cleveland. After Pancho first got lost, and then had her smash-up at Pecos, Texas, Louise Thaden had clearly been in the lead for the heavyweight planes. Phoebe Omlie, the former wing walker and flying circus performer, had been way out ahead of the others in the light plane division since day one.

But it was still up for grabs who would take second and third place among the heavy-weight planes and receive some of the $8,000 prize money. Would it be the celebrated Amelia, who had suffered mishap after mishap in this race? Or California's Gladys O'Donnell, who had up-ended her plane while departing from Wichita, but had her mechanic there in minutes filing off part of the propeller tip, before zooming off again? Or former Cleveland actress Blanche Noyes, who had had to deal with a fire, two emergency landings, and a plane repaired with tape? Or would it be New York City's Ruth Nichols, who in contrast to the others had so far flown a relatively trouble-free race?

The last leg of the race was comparatively short and easy, from Columbus to Cleveland, 120 miles over flat land. The women were given the rare treat of some free time since they were not scheduled to depart from Columbus until the afternoon. They spent that Monday morning either relaxing, or else working on their planes, having minor repairs made. Ruth Nichols was among the latter. She decided—just to be on the safe side—to take the plane up for a short test flight. But coming in, she drifted a little in the wind current and crashed into a steam-roller parked right on the runway!

Amelia, who was in a close race with Ruth Nichols for second or third place, added minutes to her time by jumping out of her own plane

· · · · · · ·

Ruth Nichols was an experienced professional flyer by the time
of the race, having flown since school days. She was the first women to fly to
every state of the union and the first woman in the world to earn an
international hydroplane license.

Ruth Nichols' plane crashed just 100 miles short of the finish line, in Columbus, Ohio. Her life was probably saved by having worn a seat belt.

· · · · · · ·

W. R. Hopkins, city manager of Cleveland, shakes hands with winner Louise Thaden at the end of the race. A proud Cliff Henderson, race manager, stands by.

· · · · · · ·

to make sure her rival was all right. Much to everyone's amazement, Ruth crawled slowly out of her upside-down plane. Saved by her seat belt, she was unhurt except for some small scratches. But her plane was wrecked. There was no way she could finish the race. Now they were down to 14 competitors out of the original 20 entrants.

A short time later, Louise Thaden zoomed in over the finish line in Cleveland in her blue and gold Travel Air. She did not realize right away she had won. But before her plane had even rolled to a stop, there were suddenly crowds of reporters swarming around her plane and pushing microphones at her. She turned off her engine, terrified of hurting people. Then, while still sitting in the cockpit, her plane was triumphantly carried over to the grandstands by a group of mechanics. She climbed out of her plane and a huge horseshoe of roses was hung around her neck. She flinched—the roses had not been de-thorned! The wreath was quickly removed and hung on the propeller of the victory plane instead. She had flown approximately 2,800 miles in 19 hours, 35 minutes.

· · · · · · ·

Louise Thaden said that the roses should hang around the nose of her plane, not on her, since it was because of her fast plane that she won.

Aeronautical Banquet
sponsored by the
Exchange Club of Columbus
honoring the fliers in the
Women's Air Derby

Sunday, August 25th, 1929
Deshler Wallick Hotel
Columbus, Ohio

Louise reacted to her win with her usual forthrightness and modesty. "All of the girls flew a splendid race, much better than I," she told reporters, adding that the only reason she won was because she happened to have a faster plane. She also announced that her trophy would be inscribed with the name of Marvel Crosson and sent to Marvel's hometown of San Diego.

Gladys O'Donnell came in second. Amelia was in third place, one and three-quarters hours after Louise, and received only $850 in prize money. Blanche with her burnt hands came in fourth. Her husband ambled over to greet her. As she saw him light up his cigar, she sharply commanded him to put it out. She had had just about enough of men and their careless smoking! In the light plane category, Phoebe Omlie came in first, as expected. Edith Foltz from the northwest came in second. Australian "Chubby" Miller came in third. As each woman landed, there were cheers and applause from the thousands of spectators gathered to watch them arrive at the Cleveland Airport.

Last to come in among the faster, heavier aircraft was Ruth Elder. As usual, she had gotten lost. She had landed in Akron, Ohio, mistaking it for Cleveland. The people in Akron told her she was in the wrong town and off she flew, only to get lost once again. This time she ran out of gas and had to make an emergency landing on a prison farm. "I've often been told I'll end up in prison, so I just wanted to see what it was like," she joked. When she finally landed in Cleveland, she, too, received an enthusiastic burst of applause. Ruth smiled broadly, happy. She was alive and in one piece and had safely finished the race.

· · · · · · ·

In Columbus, Ohio, on the final night of the race, there was a big banquet honoring the women sponsored by the local Exchange Club. Some of the women expressed sadness that the race would be soon over.

CHAPTER 10

A Sisterhood of Flyers: The Ninety-Nines

"If enough of us keep trying, we'll get someplace."

. . . .

AMELIA EARHART

Ruth's pleasure at having completed the race, even if she was last, and Louise's modest comments that the only reason she won was that she had a faster airplane were typical of the spirit of this race.

Even though many of these women had started out in a competitive frame of mind, eager to show that they were the best pilot, something changed along the way. During the course of that hard cross-country race, with all the accidents and fears of sabotage and even the death of one of them, the atmosphere changed from competitiveness to friendliness and support for each other. They developed a spirit of togetherness, and in some cases close friendship, that turned out to be more important to them than who had won or lost. Women pilots

. . . .

After the completion of the race, Amelia Earhart (holding beaker of champagne) and some of the other women in the Derby prepare to christen the Goodyear airship, The Defender.

were a rarity back then (and still are, to some extent). This was the first time that they had met other female flyers—and they enjoyed that experience. Louise Thaden told her husband when he joined her in Columbus, Ohio, at the banquet that last evening that she was sad that the race was ending. "We have helped each other, worried together, laughed over mistakes, silently wept and endured in community, recognized our strengths, and combated weakness."

As women in a field dominated by men, they not only enjoyed meeting each other, but realized that they had a lot in common. They wanted the relationships to continue after the race ended. They also realized that they would have more power to fight for equality in the skies as a group than as individuals. And they wanted to encourage more women to experience the joys of flying.

Since women pilots could compete in only a few of the races and other competitions that were held in Cleveland during the subsequent air show, they had some time to themselves. So while the men-only competitions were going on, a bunch of them had an informal meeting under the bleachers, where they talked about creating an organization of women pilots. They agreed to send out a letter inviting all licensed women pilots to come to an organizing meeting in the fall.

On November 2, 1929, many in the group, in addition to others who had not participated in the race but were nevertheless licensed pilots, met at a plane storage hangar at Curtiss Airfield on Long Island, New York. Twenty-six women pilots attended the meeting. They all agreed on the need to form an organization of their own—one to encourage women to fly and to make a united stand on the issues that affected them. Some, like Amelia, talked about the need to be able to compete as equals in men's races where they could win big money. But others thought they had a better chance to compete in women-only events.

· · · · · · ·

November 2, 1929: This first meeting of 26 women pilots would grow into today's multi-chapter, international organization of women pilots known as The Ninety-Nines. They met inside a plane hangar at Curtiss Airfield on Long Island. Fay Gillis Wells (extreme right), wearing her helmet and flight suit, poured the tea and served them cookies from a spare parts wagon. She became their first secretary. Amelia Earhart was later elected as their first president. It was just two months after the Powder Puff Derby.

They also discussed what they would call themselves. There were all kinds of suggestions, including "Sky Scrapers," "The Angels Club," and "The Climbing Vines." Amelia, still miffed over the name "Powder Puff Derby," proposed something strong and no-nonsense rather than cute. She suggested that they send out a final letter of invitation to all licensed women pilots, including some whose names were inadvertently dropped from this first meeting's list. The new group's name should be a number—the number who responded and agreed to join the first organization of women pilots. They all agreed with Amelia's suggestion. Over the following months, 99 women pilots out of the 117 licensed women pilots in the United States responded to the call—an amazingly high response rate! And so the group had a name: "The Ninety-Nines."

Years passed. The number of women pilots who joined steadily increased. Currently, there are over 6,000 licensed women pilot members from 35 countries. But the name remains the same, a legacy to those first brave women who wanted so much to fly. "The Ninety-Nines" continue to encourage women to fly by providing scholarships and information about flying to women around the world.

The National Women's Air Derby of 1929—still affectionately known as the Powder Puff Derby—was a turning point for women in aviation. It was the first transcontinental air race of its kind in which women were allowed to participate, thereby putting women on a more equal footing with men. Fourteen out of 20 of the women pilots (or 15 including Bobbi Trout, who came in a day late because of all the repair work on her plane) finished the race, a higher percentage than for any of the men's cross-country races. And a tough race it was, filled with the physical difficulties of rugged cross-country flying, the added strain of being expected to attend social events, and the the tension and potential danger from the possibility that people were tampering with their planes.

The fact that so many of these women flyers were able to overcome these problems in a calm, competent, and courageous manner greatly increased the general respect for women pilots. No doubt the public attention also inspired many other women to try flying. Fay Gillis Wells, first secretary of The Ninety-Nines, first woman to parachute from a disabled plane, and first American woman to fly a Soviet civil airplane across Russia, was one of them.

Since 1929, the all-women's cross-country race has had an on-again, off-again history. The race was not held the following year.

In 1936, Louise Thaden and Blanche Noyes teamed up to win the Bendix Transcontinental Air Race. It was the second year that women were allowed to enter. Race officials were surprised that the women not only finished the race, but won first place.

· · · · · · ·

Women pilots once again battled with an all-male race committee over the entry rules, including the committee's insistence that women could not fly the heavyweight planes with bigger engines. A number of the 1929 entrants—including Louise Thaden, Amelia Earhart, Ruth Nichols, and Blanche Noyes—boycotted the race, refusing to enter. So, the race was cancelled.

The competition was revived for a few years in the 1930s. Then in 1935, women were allowed for the first time to compete along with men in a prestigious transcontinental race for the Bendix Trophy. The very next year, in 1936, Louise Thaden and Blanche Noyes teamed up together and won! Thaden was pilot and Blanche her navigator. The sponsor had been so sure that a woman wouldn't win that he had offered $2,500 as a consolation prize to any aviatrix just able to finish the race. The race committee decided to call it a "Special Award" instead of a consolation prize, and handed that money over to Louise in addition to the winner's reward and the beautiful Bendix trophy. Another woman, Laura Ingalls, placed second.

After World War II, there were more cross-country races just for women, but they tapered off in the late 1940s. Gradually, with a name change—officially called the All-Woman Transcontinental Air Race (AWTAR)—the race regained popularity during the 1950s and 1960s. But with the energy crisis and rising fuel costs, the race in 1973 was cancelled, and the last race was held in 1977.

There is no longer a need for a race just for women. Nowadays women can participate in national races, become commercial pilots, and even become astronauts. But it all started with a race that was laughingly called the "Powder Puff Derby." By the end of the race, no one was laughing. Women had proven they could fly long distances even under the most difficult circumstances—and could hold their own with men.

· · · · · · ·

The Powder Puff Derby inspired a new generation of women pilots. During World War II, pilots called WASPS (Women Air Service Pilots) ferried B-17 bombers and other planes for the U.S. Army.

The Roaring Twenty
· · · · · · ·

The 20 pilots who participated in the first cross-country air race for women came from different backgrounds, and had equally varied levels of flying experience. But, in a time of open cockpit planes made of flimsy materials with few navigational tools and safety devices, they all shared a spirit of adventure and physical bravery. To get some idea of the peril of flying these women faced, consider these facts: Four of the twenty entrants later died in plane crashes; another two broke their backs; and one broke her arms, legs, and skull in a crash.

BARNES, FLORENCE ("PANCHO") 1901–1975

Born into a wealthy Pasadena, California, family, her grandfather was the famous Civil War balloonist, Thaddeus Lowe. She smoked cigars and wore riding jodhpurs and a beret during the race. Not only did she do stunt flying for the movies, but she organized the men stunt flyers into their first workers' union. In the late 1940s, she ran a combined bar/nightclub called the "Happy Bottom Riding Club" until the U.S. Air Force took over the property for expansion of Edwards Air Force Base.

CROSSON, MARVEL 1900–1929

She and her brother Joe built their own airplane, and later barnstormed together in California before moving on to the rugged mountains of Alaska where they ran a commercial air service. She held the women's flying record for altitude.

EARHART, AMELIA 1897-1937

Tirelessly promoted by the publicist George Putnam, she was already famous by the time of this race after being the first woman to cross the Atlantic by plane. Putnam's wife divorced him three months after the race. Amelia married him in 1931, after turning him down six times. In July 1937, she disappeared somewhere over the Pacific Ocean in her attempt to be the first woman to circle the world by plane. Expeditions still search for her missing plane.

ELDER, RUTH 1903-1977

She tried to cross the Atlantic before Amelia, but her plane plunged into the Atlantic. Her much publicized rescue combined with her glamorous good looks launched her on a movie career. She married Walter Camp, the movie producer, just after the Powder Puff Derby. She filed for divorce three years later. She was married six times, including twice to the same husband. When she died in 1977, her ashes were scattered over the Golden Gate Bridge from a plane.

FAHY, CLAIRE MAE ??-1930

Her husband, Herb, who taught her to fly, was a record-breaking test pilot. Claire died the year after the Powder Puff Derby when her planes engine failed during takeoff over Nevada. Herb was killed that same year while testing a new model plane.

FOLTZ, EDITH 1905–1956

She began her flying career as a barnstormer with her husband and was the first to land by plane in Walla Walla Valley, Washington. After the derby, she and her husband helped run the fledgling Oregon Airways. During WWII, she was one of a group of American women pilots who went over to England to join the Air Transport Auxiliary which helped ferry fighter jets for the Royal Air Force. She flew in two Powder Puff Derby races held during the 1950s.

HAIZLIP, MARY 1910–1997

She married her flying instructor, WWI aviation hero, Jim Haizlip, who ran an aviation school in Oklahoma after the war. She was just 19 during the 1929 race, the youngest of all the women pilots. In the 1930s, she came in first or second place in a number of races and set a women's speed record (255 miles per hour) that stood for seven years. In 1982, Mary was the first woman inducted into the Aviation and Space Hall of Fame.

KEITH-MILLER, JESSIE ("CHUBBIE") 1901–1972

The only Australian in the race, she was famous as the first woman to reach Australia by airplane. She had started the long flight to Australia as a passenger but by the time she had landed, she was co-piloting. Her boyfriend/co-pilot, Bill Lancaster, who taught her how to fly, was trying to make another long-distance aviation record in 1933 when his plane disappeared. In 1962, his wrecked plane and mummified remains were found in the Algerian desert.

KUNZ, OPAL 1896–1967

The socialite wife of Dr. George Frederick Kunz, a gem expert and vice president of the famous Tiffany & Co., Opal's decision to fly in the race shocked her high-society friends. But she held strong views about the need for women to achieve equality with men in aviation and said that every woman should learn to fly. Opal taught hundreds to fly during World War II. Because of her connection to Tiffany's, Tiffany jewelers designed The Ninety-Nines' badge showing interlocking nines.

NICHOLS, RUTH 1901–1960

An experienced professional flyer by the time of the race, she worked for Fairchild Airplane and Engine Company and was the first woman to fly to every state of the Union. She broke her back in a crash while piloting a transport plane in 1935, but went on in 1939 to establish the Relief Wings, a civilian air ambulance service which later was absorbed into the Civil Air Patrol during World War II. She continued to set new flight records and in 1958 set the women's records for both speed and altitude. She died in 1960, possibly by suicide.

NOYES, BLANCHE 1900–1981

A hometown favorite from Cleveland, she gave up a promising acting career to marry her husband, Dewey, a pilot in the early days of U.S. airmail and later a test pilot. Dewey bought Blanche her first plane in 1920 and then taught her how to fly it. When she got her license in July 1929, she became the first licensed woman pilot in Ohio. After her husband died in a plane crash, Blanche went to work in a U.S. government program that put markers on high places so pilots could identify their locations while flying. She won a gold medal from the Commerce Department for her 34 years of work to promote air safety.

O'DONNELL, GLADYS 1904–1973

She too learned to fly from her husband. Lloyd O'Donnell flew behind her in the Powder Puff Derby and served as her mechanic. Gladys had just received her pilot's license in 1929, and yet managed to win second place in the race. Gladys was later active in The Ninety-Nines organization of women pilots. She was also a prominent member of the Republican Party, including serving as president of the National Federation of Republican Women in 1968.

OMLIE, PHOEBE 1903–1975

A well-known barnstormer and stunt flyer, she and her husband, Vernon, had already opened a flying school by the time of the race. Phoebe Omlie, like Blanche Noyes and Louise Thaden, worked on the government program to put up markers for pilots. She also worked on air intelligence for the National Advisory Committee for Aeronautics, the forerunner of the present NASA (National Aeronautics and Space Administration).

PARIS, NEVA ??–1930

Originally from Kansas City, Missouri, she had just received her flying license in December 1920. By 1929 she had already worked in New York for the Curtis-Wright Company demonstrating their new airplanes. She was one of the main organizers of The Ninety-Nines, until she died in a plane crash just five months after the race.

PERRY, MARGARET ??–1951

She had just started flying in 1929, but already had qualified for a commercial transport license. After she recovered from the typhoid fever that hospitalized her during the race, she moved to California where she managed an airport in Culver City, perhaps the first woman to hold such a job. Margaret became the second president of The Ninety-Nines, after the death of Amelia Earhart.

RASCHE, THEA 1899–1971

She was Germany's first female stunt flyer and a well-known aerobatic flyer both in Europe and the United States. She continued to fly and write about flying back in Berlin. During WWII, her books were banned in Germany for being too pro-English/American. She then joined the Nazi Party. After the war she was tried for Nazi activities in the United States, but was acquitted.

THADEN, LOUISE 1905–1979

She dropped out of college and worked in sales for a coal company in Wichita, but grew more interested in the nearby Travel Air Company which was building airplanes. At one point in 1929, she simultaneously held the women's records for speed, altitude, and endurance (amount of time up in the air). With Blanche Noyes as her navigator, she captured first place in the 1936 Bendix cross-country race. Louise's son, daughter, and granddaughter all became pilots.

TROUT, EVELYN ("BOBBI") 1906–2003

One of the only women in the race who could be her own mechanic, she loved cars, motorcycles, and planes. She got her nickname from her bobbed (cut short) hairstyle. During World War II, she did aerial surveillance for the Los Angeles Police Department and invented a machine to sort unused rivets being scrapped by aircraft companies. After the war, she and Pancho Barnes formed the Women's Air Reserve to fly medical help to people in remote disaster zones. She died at the age of 97, the last survivor of the 1929 Powder Puff Derby. She never married.

VON MACH, MARY 1896–1980
One of the less experienced of the flyers in the 1929 derby, she went on after the race to qualify to be a flight instructor after graduating as first woman student from Parks Air College in St. Louis. During WWII, she was responsible for the final inspections of engines for B-24 bombers. In 1978, she received the Bronze Star Award from the OX-5 Pioneers for her work on the OX-5 engines and in 1987, she was inducted into the Michigan Aviation Hall of Fame.

WALKER, VERA DAWN 1897–1978
The smallest of the racers at 4 feet, 11 inches and 94 pounds, she had to sit on pillows to reach the rudder pedals. Before the race, she had been one of those daring wing-walkers and an "extra" in the movies. After the race, she became a demonstration pilot, flying to all 48 states on one sales tour to demonstrate a new engine. She quit flying in 1931 after a forced landing in the jungles of Guatemala and a subsequent illness.

Women's Firsts in Aviation

· · · · · · ·

A TIMELINE

SEPTEMBER 1910:
Blanche Scott is the first American woman to make a solo airplane flight.

APRIL 16, 1912:
Harriet Quimby, the first woman to be issued a pilot's license in the U.S., flies across the English Channel from England to France.

JUNE 15, 1921:
Bessie Coleman becomes the first African-American woman pilot after receiving an international pilot's license in France where there was less racial discrimination.

JUNE 18, 1928:
Amelia Earhart is the first woman to fly (as a passenger) across the Atlantic Ocean.

DECEMBER 20, 1928:
Viola Gentry is the first woman to attempt a women's endurance record for the most time spent in the air, at eight hours, six minutes, 37 seconds.

APRIL 13, 1929:
Louise Thaden sets women's speed record when she flies at 156 miles per hour.

MAY 28, 1929:
Marvel Crosson sets women's altitude record when she flies 24,000 feet over Los Angeles.

AUGUST 18-26, 1929:
Fourteen out of 20 women successfully complete the first cross-country air race for women known as the "Powder Puff Derby."

SEPTEMBER 1, 1929:
Fay Gillis is the first woman to jump using a parachute from a disabled aircraft thereby saving her life.

NOVEMBER 2, 1929:
First meeting of The Ninety-Nines, an organization of women pilots.

SEPTEMBER 4, 1936:
Louise Thaden and Blanche Noyes, as co-pilots, win the Bendix Trophy in a New York to Los Angeles cross-country race.

JULY 1937:
Amelia Earhart disappears over the Pacific Ocean while attempting to be the first woman to fly around the world.

SEPTEMBER 23, 1938:
Jacqueline Cochran wins the Bendix Trophy (Burbank, California, to Cleveland non-stop).

JUNE 10, 1942:
U.S. Army announces creation of Women's Auxiliary Ferrying Squadron (WAFS) so that women can ferry airplanes to American pilots.

SUMMER OF 1943:
WAFS combines with another group to form the more well-known WASPs—Women Airforce Service Pilots—to ferry planes to air bases and ports, help train bomber pilots, and test fighter planes. They are not allowed to fly in combat zones.

MAY 18, 1953:
Jacqueline Cochran is the first woman to break the sound barrier while piloting a North American F-86 Sabre jet plane.

JUNE 16, 1963:
Valentina Tereshkova, a Russian, becomes the first woman in space.

FEBRUARY 1968:
Gillian Cazalet of Britain becomes the first woman to pilot a commercial airline.

JUNE 1983:
Dr. Sally Ride is the first American woman in space.

JULY 1984:
Soviet cosmonaut Svetlana Savitskaya becomes the first female to walk in space.

FEBRUARY 1995:
Eileen Collins becomes the first woman to pilot a space shuttle.

SEPTEMBER 1996:
Shannon Lucid sets space endurance record for women—and for American men as well—after returning from six months in a Russian space station.

JULY 1999:
Eileen Collins is the first woman to fly as a space shuttle commander.

Bibliography

· · · · · · ·

BOOKS AND PERIODICALS:

Abels, Jules. *In the Time of Silent Cal.* New York: G.P. Putnam's Sons, 1969.

Allen, Frederick Lewis. *Only Yesterday: An Informal History of the 1920s.* New York: Harper & Row, 1931.

Andrews, Melodie. "Daredevils and Ladybirds: Gender and the Aviation Industry before World War II," Essays in *Economics and Business Histories*, 1995.

Atkins, Jeannine. *Wings and Rockets: The Story of Women in Air and Space.* New York: Farrar, Straus & Giroux, 2003.

Cleveland *Plain Dealer.*

Corn, Joseph J. *The Winged Gospel: America's Romance with Aviation.* New York: Oxford University Press, 1983.

Day, Leon. "Powder Puff Problems and the Curse of the Lady Birds" in *Minerva Magazine*, summer 1993, Volume XI, no. 2.

Douglas, George H. *Women of the 20s.* Dallas: Saybrook Publishers, 1986.

Edwards Air Force Base, History Office. "Pancho Barnes, An Original," March 2, 1982. Papers available at Smithsonian Air & Space Museum archives.

Jablonski, Edward. *Man with Wings: A Pictorial History of Aviation.* Garden City, New York: Doubleday and Company, 1980.

Jessen, Gene Nora. *The Powder Puff Derby of 1929.* Naperville, Illinois: Sourcebooks, 2002.

Kessler, Lauren. *The Happy Bottom Riding Club: The Life and Times of Pancho Barnes.* New York: Random House, 2000.

Leinwald, Gerald. *High Tide of the 1920s: 1927.* New York: Four Walls Eight Windows, 2001.

Los Angeles Times.

Lovell, Mary S. *The Sound of Wings: The Life of Amelia Earhart.* New York: St. Martins Press, 1989.

McMullen, Frances Drewry, interview with Amelia Earhart which appeared in *The Woman's Journal*, October 1929.

The New York Times.

Pazmany-Brooks, Kathleen. *United States Women in Aviation, 1919-1929.* Washington, D.C.: Smithsonian Institution Press, 1991.

Sloat, Warren. *1929: America Before the Crash.* New York: Macmillan, 1979.

Tate, Grover Ted. *The Lady Who Tamed Pegasus: The Story of Pancho Barnes.* Maverick, 1984.

Thaden, Louise. *High, Wide, and Frightened.* New edition, Fayetteville, Arkansas: University of Arkansas Press, 2004.

Thaden, Louise. "The National Women's Air Derby" article in *Aviation Quarterly.*

Veczey, George & Dale, George C. *The Pioneers of Aviation Speak for Themselves.* New York: E.P. Dutton, 1979.

WEB SITES:

About later women's races,
www.aerofiles.com/powderpuff.html
www.hickoksports.com/historypowdpuff.shtml#hist1

Formation of The Ninety-Nines as well as on the race of 1929,
www.ninety-nines.org

"Women in Air Racing"
www.pilotfriend.com/century-of-flight

About Jesse "Chubby" Keith-Miller and other women pilots, "The Pioneers"
www.ctie.monash.edu.au/hargrave/miller.html

About Mary von Mach,
www.michiganaviation.org/enshrinees/Bios/vonmach.html

Interview with Bobbi Trout,
www.avweb.com/articles/profiles/btrout/

Resource Guide

· · · · · · ·

OTHER BOOKS ABOUT WOMEN PILOTS

Most of the following books about women pilots are writ-ten for adults, but might interest younger readers as well. Those with an asterisk are specifically aimed at younger readers:

*Atkins, Jeannine. Wings and Rockets: The Story of Women in Air and Space. New York: Farrar, Straus & Giroux, 2003.

Boase, Wendy. The Sky's The Limit. New York: Macmillan Publishing Company, 1979.

Brooks-Pazmany, Kathleen. United States Women in Aviation 1919-1929. Washington, D.C.: Smithsonian Institution Press, 1991.

Jessen, Gene Nora. The Powder Puff Derby of 1929. Naperville, Illinois: Sourcebooks, 2002.

*Nathan, Amy. Yankee Doodle Gals, Women Pilots of World War II. Washington, D.C.: National Geographic Society, 2001.

Rich, Doris. Amelia Earhart: A Biography. Washington, D.C.: Smithsonian Institution Press, 1989.

Smith, Elinor. Aviatrix. New York: Harcourt Brace Jovanovich, 1981.

Thaden, Louise. High, Wide, and Frightened. New edition, Fayetteville, Arkansas: University of Arkansas Press, 2004.

WEB SITES

The Ninety-Nines
www.ninety-nines.org

Women in Aviation
www.women-in-aviation.com

International Forest of Friendship
www.IFOF.org

PLACES TO VISIT

Amelia Earhart Birthplace Museum, Atchison, Kansas: The Ninety-Nines are fully restoring the 1850s structure to look like it did when Amelia lived there as a child.

International Forest of Friendship, Atchison, Kansas: Co-founded by the late Fay Gillis Wells in 1994, one of the original members of The Ninety-Nines, it is a living, growing memorial—trees—planted in honor of those who contributed to the field of aviation. Among the trees is the so-called "Moon Tree" grown from a seed taken to the moon by the Apollo 14 crew, which honors the 17 astronauts who gave their lives in America's pioneering space programs.

International Women's Air & Space Museum
Burke Lakefront Airport
1501 North Marginal Road
Cleveland, Ohio 44114
With ongoing exhibits and special events honoring female pilots and astronauts, this museum has continued to expand since it first opened in 1986. For a preview, visit its Web site at http://www.iwasm.org/index.php.

National Air and Space Museum, Smithsonian Institution, Washington, D.C.: You can see one of Amelia Earhart's airplanes there and an exhibit on early women flyers.

The Ninety-Nines Museum of Women Pilots
4300 Amelia Earhart Road
Oklahoma City, Oklahoma 73159
Located on the second floor of the organization's head-quarters, the museum contains displays and artifacts focusing on the history of women in aviation. There are also archives and research resources maintained on the site.

Sources

· · · · · · ·

One of my first sources of information about the Powder Puff Derby was the 1991 book published by the Smithsonian Institution, *United States Women in Aviation 1919-1929*, written by Kathleen Brooks-Pazmany.

My other main source was newspapers of that time, especially those published during the days of the race in 1929, mainly *The New York Times*, Cleveland *Plain Dealer*, and the *Los Angeles Times*.

A more recent, and invaluable, source of information, especially about what happened to the women pilots who participated in that race many years later, is Gene Nora Jessen's wonderful 2002 book entitled, *The Powder Puff Derby of 1929*.

I also gained information from interviews I conducted with Doris Rich about Amelia Earhart, and the late Fay Gillis Wells about what flying was like in the early days. The interviews were filmed for a cable television program called *Out of the Past* that I hosted many years ago. Ed Cooney was the director, and my interviews were aired on the Fairfax Public Access station in the 1990s.

PROLOGUE
Amelia Earhart quote, p. 1, is from an interview with Amelia Earhart by Frances Drewry McMullen in *The Woman's Journal*, October 1929, p.10.

THE "ROARING" TWENTIES
Song stanza on p. 5 from the song "Ain't We Got Fun." Words and music by Gus Kahn, Raymond B. Egan, & Richard Whiting, 1921. Material on this general historical period, as well as about aviation and about women during the 1920s, came mainly from the following four sources: Jules Abels' *In the Time of Silent Cal*; Frederick Allen's *Only Yesterday: An Informal History of the 1920s*; George H. Douglas' *Women of the 20s*; and Warren Sloat's *1929: America Before the Crash*. Material on women's role in WWI and the "yeomanettes" came primarily from an article by Jean Gillette entitled "Uncle Sam's First Women

Recruits" in *The Retired Officer Magazine* (July 1991). The article was sent to me by my mother-in-law, the late Rita Connelly Blair, a military officer's wife. Information about the women's flight records came from Kathleen Pazmany-Brooks' wonderful book, *United States Women in Aviation*, pp. 30-32.

THE RULES OF THE RACE
Cleveland air show information came mainly from an article on "Cleveland Air Races" on the following Web site: http://www.pilotfriend.com/century-of-flight. Information about pre-race disagreements came from newspapers of the day, particularly from the Cleveland *Plain Dealer*, and from Doris Rich's excellent book *Amelia Earhart: A Biography*, on pp. 89-90. The problem of Hollywood starlets pretending to be pilots; Fay Gillis' jump with a parachute; and rules of the race came from the Pazmany-Brooks' book, already cited. What Amelia took with her came from Amelia's interview with Frances Drewry, already cited.

WHO ENTERED—AND WHY
Information about Amelia Earhart's motivations came from my interview with Doris Rich and from a book by Edward Jablonski entitled *Man with Wings: A Pictorial History of Aviation*. Information about Ruth Elder came mainly from the newspapers of the time. Stories about Pancho Barnes came from Grover Ted Tate's book, *The Lady Who Tamed Pegasus: The Story of Pancho Barnes* and Lauren Kessler's book, *The Happy Bottom Riding Club: The Life and Times of Pancho Barnes*. Louise Thaden, from her own memoir, *High, Wide, and Frightened*; Chubby Keith-Miller and Ruth Nichols, from the Brooks-Pazmany book; Marvel Crosson from newspapers of the day; Bobbi Trout stories from her obituary in *The New York Times*.

AND THEY'RE OFF!
Male reporter's quote from Lauren Kessler's book, already cited, p.71 Will

Rogers' quip about Calvin Coolidge from Gerald Leinwald's book, *High Tide of the 1920s: 1927*. Will Rogers' quote about it being a "Powder Puff Derby" from Gene Nora Jessen's wonderfully detailed book, *The Powder Puff Derby of 1929*, p. 66. Amelia Earhart's mechanical troubles and bad landing from Jeannine Atkins' book for younger readers, *Wings and Rockets, The Story of Women in Air and Space*, pp.52-54. Discussion of Pancho Barnes' movie work from the Lauren Kessler book. The fight over changing the airfield from Calexico to Yuma I gleaned mainly from newspaper accounts.

SABOTAGE?
Both of Pancho Barnes' quotes from Grover Ted Tate's book, already cited, p. 46. Louise Thaden discussed the telegram warning of sabotage in her memoir, *High, Wide, and Frightened*, p.46 in the University of Arkansas edition. Thea Rasche's remarks from the Cleveland *Plain Dealer* of the days of the race. Ruth Elder's remark in Jessen's *The Powder Puff Derby of 1929*, p. 94. Claire Fahy's charges reported by Associated Press in the *Los Angeles Times*, August 20, 1929. Information on sabotage investigation from the *Los Angeles Times*, world edition, August 21-22, 1929. Jessie Keith-Miller's quote, as reported by Leon Day in his article "Powder Puff Problems and the Curse of the Lady Birds" in *Minerva Magazine*. Bobbi Trout and Louise Thaden's problems with sabotage from Leon Day's 1993 article, too.

TRAGEDY ON DAY THREE
Louise Thaden's observations from her memoir, *High, Wide, and Frightened*. Speculations about Marvel Crosson becoming ill or having her period from Melodie Andrews' article, "Daredevils and Ladybirds: Gender and the Aviation Industry before World War II" in the 1995 *Essays in Economics and Business Histories*. Details about Marvel Crosson's death and the aftermath as reported in

The New York Times during those days of the race. Halliburton and El Pasco newspaper saying race should be stopped from Louise Thaden's article, "The National Women's Air Derby" in *Aviation Quarterly*, p. 164. Louise Thaden quote from her memoir, *High, Wide, and Frightened*, p.51.

TROUBLES IN TEXAS
Louise Thaden's and Gladys O'Donnell's teary reaction to Marvel's death comes from Doris Rich's book, p.92. Pancho's being voted out from McMullen interview with Amelia Earhart, previously cited. Accounts of Blanche Noyes' fire from news accounts of the race. Louise Thaden's reaction to Blanche's landing from Louise Thaden's memoirs, *High, Wide, and Frightened*, pp.

54-55. Other pilots' troubles in Texas were taken from newspaper accounts.

"PLEASE GOD, LET THEM ALL BE COWS!"
Ruth Elder's quote, her story of landing among the cows, and the announcement of her marriage plans were taken mainly from newspaper accounts during the race.

TROUBLES ALL THE WAY THROUGH TO THE END!
Continuing troubles of the women pilots culled mainly from newspaper accounts during the race. Amelia's adding time to her race to make sure Ruth Nichols was all right comes from Atkins' book, *Wings and Rockets*, p. 71. Louise Thaden quoted in

her memoir, *High, Wide, and Frightened*, p. 59. Accounts of Louise Thaden's finish come mainly from the Brooks-Pasmany book and Louise Thaden's memoir. Ruth Elder quoted in the Cleveland *Plain Dealer*, August 27, 1929.

A SISTERHOOD OF FLYERS: THE NINETY-NINES
Louise Thaden quoted in Gene Nora Jessen's *The Powder Puff Derby of 1929*, p.190. Information on the formation of The Ninety-Nines and Amelia Earhart's opening quote comes from their Web site, www.ninety-nines.org. Story about the women pilots' first informal meeting under the bleachers at the Cleveland air races from an interview with Bobbi Trout, ww.avweb.com.

Illustrations Credits

· · · · · · ·

Abbreviations: International Women's Air & Space Museum (IWASM); National Air and Space Museum/Smithsonian Institution (NASM/SI).

Cover (Foreground), AP/Wide World Photos; cover (Background), NASM/SI (SI 97-16493); Back Cover, NASM/SI (SI 97-16493);

Page: 1, Illustration by David M. Seager; 2-3, NASM/SI (SI 83-2117); 7, Thaden Family Collection; 8, NASM/SI (SI 83-2108); 10, Library of Congress; 11, Underwood & Underwood/CORBIS; 13, NASM/SI (SI 79-6362); 16, Bettmann/CORBIS; 19, IWASM; 20, Library of Congress; 23, Minnesota Historical Society/CORBIS; 24 - 25, Bettmann/CORBIS; 26, National Archives; 27, NASM/SI (SI 79-12296); 29, Bettmann/CORBIS; 30, National Archives; 32, NASM/SI (SI 2005-21622); 33, IWASM; 34 (upper), IWASM; 34 (lower left), IWASM; 34 (lower right), NASM/SI (SI 93-15838); 35, IWASM; 36, NASM/SI (SI 2005-21623); 38, Bettmann/CORBIS; 41, National Archives; 42, AP/Wide World Photos; 45, NASM/SI (SI 83-2145); 46, NASM/SI (SI 75-4503); 48, Bettmann/CORBIS; 50, Bettmann/CORBIS; 52, Library of Congress; 53, Bettmann/CORBIS; 54, NASM/SI (SI 83-2116); 56, Library of Congress; 57, Underwood & Underwood/CORBIS; 59, Underwood & Underwood/Corbis; 60 (both), The Everett Collection, Inc.; 62 (upper), The San Bernardino Sun; 62 (center), The San Bernardino Sun; 62 (lower left), The Plain Dealer; 62 (lower right), The New York Times; 64, NASM/SI (SI 2005-7751); 65, IWASM; 66, The 99s Museum of Women Pilots; 69, NASM/SI (SI 83-2103); 70, IWASM; 72 - 73, NASM/SI (SI 79-6363); 74 - 75, Library of Congress; 77 (left), The Plain Dealer; 77 (right), IWASM; 78, CORBIS; 81, National Archives; 82 - 83, NASM/SI (SI 79-10578); 84, NASM/SI (SI 2005-7752); 85, AP/Wide World Photos; 86, CORBIS; 88 - 89, NASM/SI (SI 89-21975); 90, Underwood & Underwood/CORBIS; 92, NASM/SI (SI 73-567); 94 (left), AP/Wide World Photos; 94 - 95, NASM/SI (SI 2005-7750); 97, AP/Wide World Photos; 98 - 99, AP/Wide World Photos; 100, NASM/SI (SI 83-2146); 101, NASM/SI (SI 83-2133); 102 (lower left), IWASM; 102 - 103, IWASM; 104, National Archives; 106 -107, NASM/SI (SI 2005-7753); 109, NASM/SI (SI 77-4170); 110 -111, National Museum of the U.S. Air Force; 112 (upper), NASM/SI (SI 84-10315); 112 (lower), Bettmann/CORBIS; 113 (upper), Bettmann/CORBIS; 113 (center), Bettmann/CORBIS; 113 (lower), The 99s Museum of Women Pilots; 114 (upper), NASM/SI (SI 2005-21624); 114 (center), AP/Wide World Photos; 114 (lower), NASM/SI (SI 2005-7752); 115 (upper), The 99s Museum of Women Pilots; 115 (lower), AP/Wide World Photos; 116 (upper), Bettmann/CORBIS; 116 (lower), NASM/SI (SI 83-2103); 117 (upper), National Archives; 117 (center), NASM/SI (SI 79-9684); 117 (lower), AP/Wide World Photos; 118 (upper), NASM/SI (SI 79-5904); 118 (center), NASM/SI (SI 83-2121); 118 (lower), NASM/SI (SI 83-2101); 119 (upper), IWASM; 119 (lower), AP/Wide World Photos.

Index

· · · · · · ·

PUBLISHED BY THE NATIONAL GEOGRAPHIC SOCIETY

John M. Fahey, Jr.,
President and Chief Executive Officer

Gilbert M. Grosvenor,
Chairman of the Board

Nina D. Hoffman,
Executive Vice President, President Books and Education Publishing Group

Ericka Markman,
Senior Vice President, President of Children's Books and Education Publishing Group

Stephen Mico,
Publisher, Vice President of Children's Books and Education Publishing Group

STAFF FOR THIS BOOK

Nancy Laties Feresten,
Vice President, Editor-in-Chief of Children's Books

Bea Jackson,
Design Director, Children's Books and Education Publishing Group

Margaret Sidlosky,
Illustrations Director, Children's Books and Education Publishing Group

Jennifer Emmett,
Project Editor

David M. Seager,
Designer

Annette Kiesow,
Illustrations Editor

Priyanka Lamichhane,
Editorial Assistant

Jean Cantu, Aaron Hubbard
Illustrations Assistants

Carl Mehler,
Director of Maps

Stuart Armstrong, Gregory Ugiansky, and XNR Productions,
Map Research and Production

Rebecca E. Hinds,
Managing Editor

R. Gary Colbert,
Production Director

Lewis R. Bassford,
Production Manager

Vincent P. Ryan,
Manufacturing Manager

The world's largest nonprofit scientific and educational organization, the National Geographic Society was founded in 1888 "for the increase and diffusion of geographic knowledge." Since then it has supported scientific exploration and spread information to its more than eight million members worldwide. The National Geographic Society educates and inspires millions every day through magazines, books, television programs, videos, maps and atlases, research grants, the National Geographic Bee, teacher workshops, and innovative classroom materials. The Society is supported through membership dues and income from the sale of its educational products. Members receive NATIONAL GEOGRAPHIC magazine—the Society's official journal—discounts on Society products and other benefits. For more information about the National Geographic Society, its educational programs and publications, and ways to support its work, please call 1-800-NGS-LINE (647-5463) or write to the following address:

National Geographic Society
1145 17th Street N.W.
Washington, D.C. 20036-4688
U.S.A.

Visit the Society's Web site at www.nationalgeographic.com